Family & Parenthood Policy & Practice

Single lone mothers:
problems, prospects and policies

Louie Burghes
with Mark Brown

PUBLISHED BY

Family Policy Studies Centre

SUPPORTED BY

JR
JOSEPH ROWNTREE FOUNDATION

Published by Family Policy Studies Centre,
231 Baker Street, London NW1 7XE.
Tel: 0171 486 8179

ISBN 0 907051 84 7

November 1995

The **Family Policy Studies Centre** is an
independent body which analyses family trends and
the impact of policy. It is a centre of research and
information. The Centre's Governing Council
represents a wide spectrum of political opinion, as
well as professional, academic, church, local authority
and other interests. The facts presented and views
expressed in this report are those of the author and
not necessarily those of the Centre.

The **Joseph Rowntree Foundation** has supported
this project as part of its programme of research and
innovative development projects, which it hopes will
be of value to policy makers and practitioners. The
facts presented and views expressed in this report,
however, are those of the authors and not necessarily
those of the Foundation.

SUPPORTED BY

JR
JOSEPH
ROWNTREE
FOUNDATION

Design and print by Intertype

Contents

Acknowledgements

I am most grateful to those who helped us with this report. They include, first and foremost, the mothers and young women who were interviewed as part of the qualitative research. I would also like to thank the Joseph Rowntree Foundation and the members of the JRF Advisory Committee, my colleagues at the FPSC, the qualitative research team at SCPR and Charlie Owen and David Utting.

Introduction

This report is about single, lone mothers – women who have never been married and who live alone with their dependent children. As a sub-group, they arguably exhibit more diversity than any other category of lone parent. Their average age is around 25 years, but they include both teenage mothers whose conceptions were unplanned and older women who may have taken a positive decision to have a child on their own. Significantly, the description 'single lone mother' also applies to women who have never been married and who have no current resident partner, but who have had a cohabiting relationship in which their children were conceived, born and/or lived. They are indistinguishable in national lone parent statistics from those who have never cohabited, yet may have very different characteristics. The social and economic circumstances of these mothers may also differ. From a policy-making perspective, it is important to understand how and why.

Demographic background

The total number of single lone mothers has risen fivefold in 20 years. In 1992 there were estimated to be 490 thousand caring for more than half a million dependent children.[1](Table 1)

Table 1	'Best estimates' of the number of lone parent families				
Great Britain					**thousands**
Family type	1971	1976	1986	1991	1992*
Single mothers	90	130	230	440	490
Separated mothers	170	185	190	260	300
Divorced mothers	120	230	410	430	430
Widowed mothers	120	115	80	70	60
All mothers	500	660	910	1200	1280
All fathers	70	90	100	100	120
All lone parents	570	750	1010	1300	1400

*Provisional

Source: John Haskey (1994).

Single lone mothers accounted for just over one in three lone parents in 1992 compared with one in six in 1971 (Table 2). They have grown, too, as a proportion of all families with dependent children – to more than seven per cent from one per cent in the early 1970s.[2]

Table 2	Proportions of lone parent families				
Great Britain					**percentages**
Family type	1971	1976	1986	1991	1992*
Single mothers	15.8	17.3	22.8	33.8	35.0
Separated mothers	29.8	24.7	18.8	20.0	21.4
Divorced mothers	21.0	30.7	40.6	33.0	30.7
Widowed mothers	21.0	15.3	7.9	5.4	4.3
All mothers	87.6	88.0	90.1	92.2	91.4
All fathers	12.3	12.0	9.9	7.7	8.6
All lone parents	100.0	100.0	100.0	100.0	100.0

*Provisional

Percentages may not add to 100 because of rounding.

Source: Calculated from John Haskey (1994).

Single lone motherhood is not necessarily a static state. John Ermisch suggested on the basis of a 1980 survey that single lone mothers tend to leave lone parenthood more rapidly than separated or divorced lone parents – an average of less than three years and five years respectively.[3] More recently, a survey by Jonathan Bradshaw and Jane Millar found there was little difference in the average length of time spent as a lone parent between single and previously married lone parents. Shorter spells were, however, recorded by those who had been cohabiting when they became pregnant. The average time spent as a lone parent was just under four years (44 months).[4]

Policy background

Single lone motherhood is not merely more common, but also far more visible as a policy issue than it was 20 years ago. This is partly due to the social security costs with which it is associated.[5] More than eight out of ten single lone mothers, for example, receive Income Support compared with seven out of ten lone parents overall. Some, because of their age, receive a lower rate of Income Support.[6] Single lone mothers are, in addition, less likely to be receiving maintenance payments for their children. Where they do, the amounts are generally smaller than those received by other lone parents. They are also more likely to live in local authority rented accommodation.[7]

Fears are sometimes expressed that the recent growth in the number of single lone mothers is not only expensive to taxpayers, but also represents a rejection of two-parent family life. Yet the fact that there has been a sharp increase in the number of never married women bringing up children does not necessarily mean that they planned things that way. Actual circumstances may be a poor guide to attitudes and aspirations regarding family life. Nor, can it be assumed that because women currently fit the definition of a single lone mother that they will always be living without a partner or parenting alone.

Aims of the project

The present project, accordingly, had four principal aims:

- to explore the demographic development of single lone motherhood;

- to describe the socio-economic circumstances of single lone mothers and their sub-groups and compare them with all lone parents;

- to explore the underlying influences on single lone motherhood;

- to draw policy implications from the findings.

In addition to a review of existing literature, the research included a detailed analysis of available demographic data and an in-depth 'qualitative' survey of young mothers. The latter compared the experiences and attitudes of single lone mothers with those of mothers who were cohabiting when they were interviewed but who had been 'at risk' of single lone motherhood when they conceived. Further comparisons were possible through interviews with a small group of single teenagers who were childless but sexually active.

Structure of the report

The report is divided into two parts. Part I explores the **demographic trends** in single lone motherhood (chapter 2) and its **social and economic characteristics** (chapter 3). Part II contains the findings of the qualitative investigation of young motherhood beginning with an introduction (chapter 4). The findings from this research are presented under five broad themes: **'Sexual experience and conception'** (chapter 5); **'Pregnancy'** (chapter 6); **'Relationships'** (chapter 7); **'Motherhood'** (chapter 8) and **'Work and family'** (chapter 9). The paper ends with concluding comments and a consideration of policy issues (chapter 10). There are two appendices, **'Methodological notes on the qualitative research'** and **'Additional information from the research'.**

Notes

1   Haskey, J. (1994).

2   ibid.

3   Ermisch, J. (1989).

4   Bradshaw, J. and Millar, J. (1991). Actual average durations may have been overestimated as shorter durations were thought to be under represented in the survey.

5   Department of Social Security (1993) and (1994).

6   Chapter 3 and Burghes, L. (1993).

7   Chapter 3 and Burghes, L. (1993).

Part I
Statistical Profile

Demographic trends

Mark Brown

This chapter explores the demographic background to the increase in single lone motherhood of the last 25 years. In so doing, it assesses connections between the increase and the sharp rise in the proportion of conceptions and births that have taken place outside marriage. More particularly, it examines the two main pathways by which women come to be classified as single lone mothers[1] and the contribution that each has made to growth in the headline total.

Trends in motherhood outside marriage

The preliminary aim is to establish recent trends in births to the never-married. Unfortunately this cannot be done directly from OPCS birth data which is not broken down fully by marital status.

Consequently, the analysis starts with data for all unmarried women from which births to the never-married are estimated.

Conceptions

Conception rates both inside and outside marriage followed a similar pattern during the 1970s of a fall followed by a modest increase. In the 1980s, however, they diverged (Figure 1). While the rate for married women remained constant, that for unmarried women rose markedly, before dipping slightly in 1991.

As a result of this trend and the declining marriage rate, the proportion of all conceptions

Figure 1   **Conception rates, by marital status. England and Wales 1971-1991.**

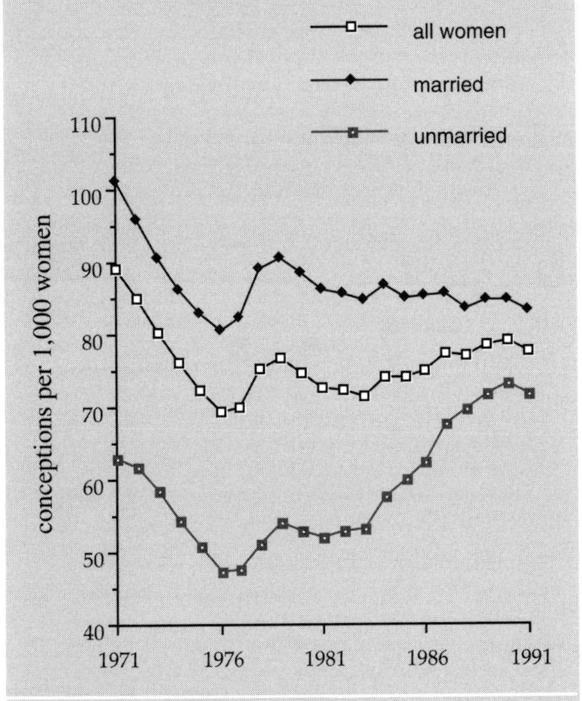

Source: OPCS (1987) and (1994a).

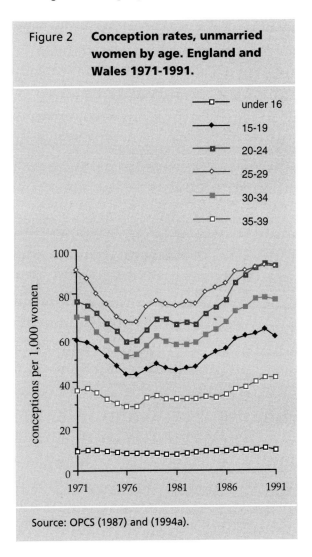

Figure 2   **Conception rates, unmarried women by age. England and Wales 1971-1991.**

Source: OPCS (1987) and (1994a).

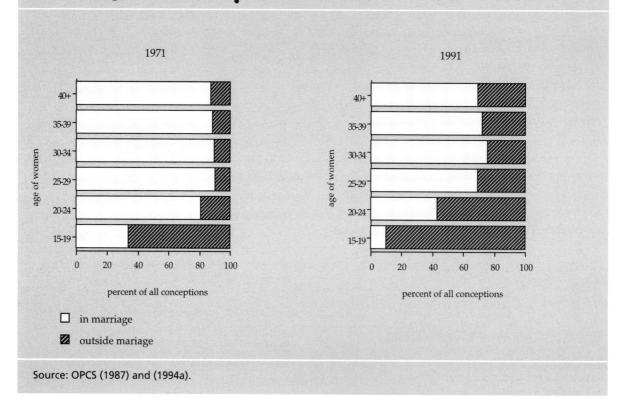

Figure 3   All conceptions, proportion occurring in and out of marriage, by age of women. England and Wales 1971 and 1991.

Source: OPCS (1987) and (1994a).

occurring outside marriage reached 44 per cent in 1991 – double the percentage 20 years earlier.

The conception rate outside marriage increased for all age groups during this period with the exception of girls under 16 (Figure 2). However, nine out of 10 conceptions to women under 20 are extra-marital – a higher proportion than for any other age group. (Figure 3).

Nevertheless, the statistics also show that the total number of teenage conceptions outside marriage each year has been in decline since rising to a peak in 1987[2] (Box 1). Younger women also account for a smaller percentage of extra-marital conceptions – down from nearly half at the beginning of the 1970s to around a quarter at the beginning of the 1990s (Figure 4).

Note on the use of data

The chapter uses OPCS data from two different statistical points of reference:

- **conceptions and their outcomes;**
- **live births.**

*Linking these two data sources presents problems for a number of reasons:

i) **Conception outcomes are based on the age of the mother at the time of the conception. The month of conception is not provided in the data. Thus, there is no way of telling whether a woman aged 19 who conceived in 1990 gave birth (or had an abortion) in 1990 when she was still 19 or 1991 when she was aged 20. This discrepancy partly explains why figures for the total number of live births for a given year is unlikely to be the same as that given for the total number of conceptions leading to 'maternities'.**

ii) **Outcomes enumerated by the conception statistics include 'terminations' and 'maternities'. A maternity indicates a pregnancy which continued to term, but it is not always the same thing as a 'live birth' in the birth statistics. Some maternities end in still births and others in multiple live births.**

*These points need to be borne in mind when reading this chapter, which in places makes combined use of conception data and live birth data. This is clearly not a ideal state of affairs. The pre-birth information which the conception data alone provides can, nevertheless, cast valuable light on trends in lone parenthood.

Single lone mothers: problems, prospects and policies

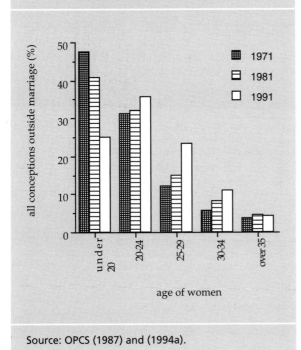

Figure 4   All out-of-marriage conceptions, proportion by age group. England and Wales 1971, 1981 and 1991.

Source: OPCS (1987) and (1994a).

Outcomes of conceptions outside marriage

By no means all those unmarried women who conceive will go on to give birth as single lone mothers. Some will miscarry or have their pregnancy terminated, while others will be cohabiting or married by the time their babies are born. Figure 5 does not distinguish between extra-marital births where mothers are cohabiting and those where they are single. But it does demonstrate the rapidly diminishing proportion of conceptions leading to so-called 'shotgun' marriages – just nine per cent in 1991 compared with 36 per cent in 1971.

Table 1, meanwhile, shows that conceptions to teenagers are especially unlikely to lead to marriage compared with 20 years ago. It is also observable that the proportion of teenage, extra-marital conceptions leading to abortion is somewhat lower than in 1981. Extra-marital births were the outcomes of 57 per cent such pregnancies in 1991 – virtually double the proportion in 1971.

However, teenage mothers actually make up a smaller proportion of current births to unmarried mothers today then in the 1970s and the overall number of teenage mothers (married and unmarried) has fallen significantly in recent decades (see Box 1).

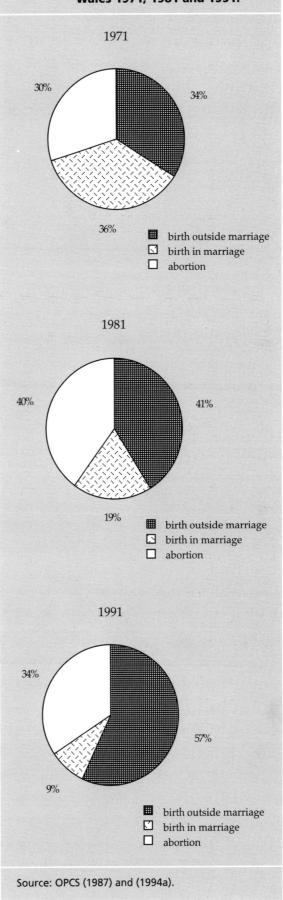

Figure 5   Conceptions outside marriage. Outcomes as a proportion of conceptions. England and Wales 1971, 1981 and 1991.

Source: OPCS (1987) and (1994a).

Table 1   Conceptions outside marriage. Outcomes as a proportion of conceptions by age of women at conception. England and Wales 1971, 1981 and 1991.

	1971 %			1981 %			1991 %		
	outside	inside	termination	outside	inside	termination	outside	inside	termination
all ages	34	36	30	41	19	40	57	9	34
under 16	44	19	37	38	5	57	48	1	51
under 20	29	45	26	39	20	41	57	5	38
20-24	33	34	33	41	20	39	57	9	35
25-29	44	22	34	44	18	36	58	10	31
30-34	49	17	34	42	19	39	59	11	30
35-39	50	13	38	39	13	49	55	11	34
over 40	48	12	40	30	8	63	43	7	50

Source: OPCS (1987) and (1994a).

Figure 6 plots the increase in the overall rate and numbers of extra-marital conceptions leading to maternities outside marriage.[3]

The births to unmarried women in Figure 6 include those to the separated, divorced and widowed, as well as those to the never-married. In the absence of direct data, the number of births to the never-married only have to be estimated and we have used Jacqui Cooper's work to do so.[4] The result (Figure 7) provides estimates of the annual additions, by age, to the stock of never-married mothers who may be single lone or cohabiting mothers.

Figure 6   Conceptions outside marriage, by outcome (rates and total numbers). England and Wales 1971-1991.

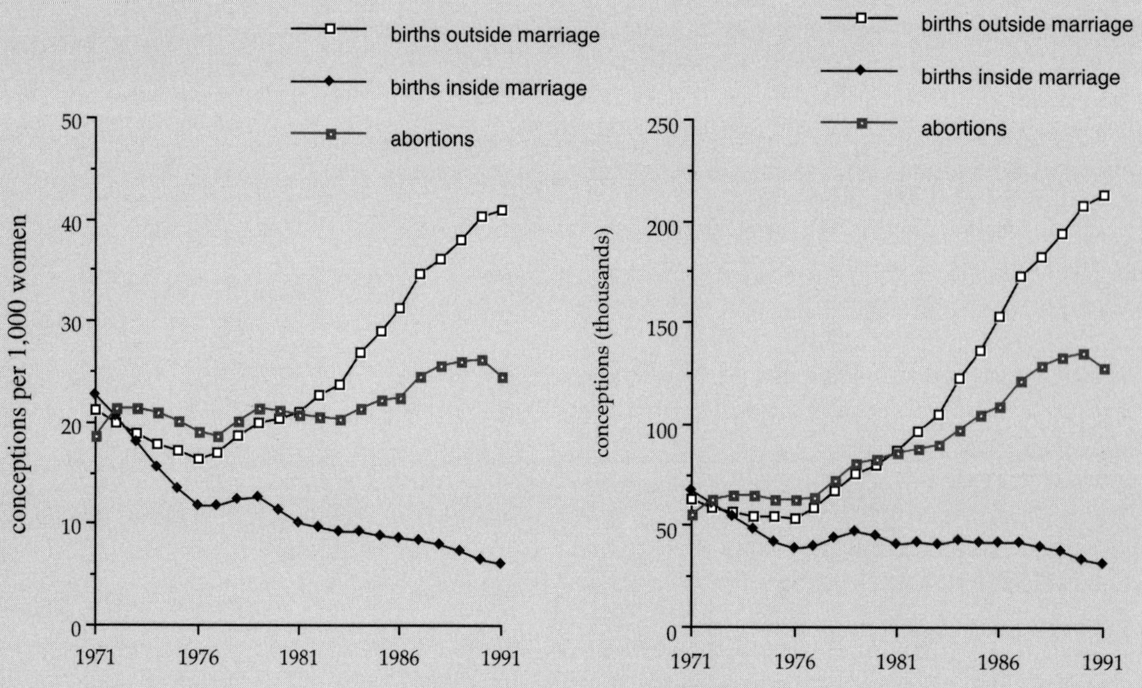

Source: OPCS (1987) and (1994a).

Single lone mothers: problems, prospects and policies

Figure 7 Estimates of the annual additions, by age, to the stock of never-maried mothers.

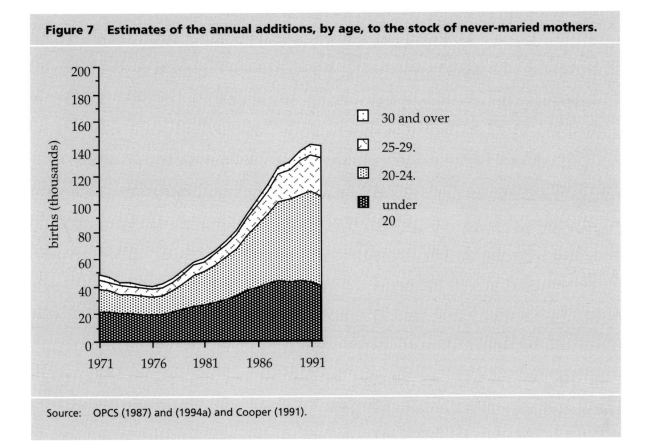

Source: OPCS (1987) and (1994a) and Cooper (1991).

BOX 1   A crisis of teenage motherhood?

- **The 1980s witnessed increases in the rate and number of out of marriage maternities conceived by teenage women. This was in sharp contrast to reductions in teenage fertility in Europe.[5]**

- **There were, even so, more than 10,000 *fewer* maternities (inside and outside marriage) to teenage women in 1991 than in 1981 – and 42,000 fewer than in 1971. (Figure 8)**

- **In 1971 there were 67.3 maternities per 1,000 teenage women compared with 40.4 per 1,000 in 1992.[6]**

Figure 8   **Trends in maternities for women who conceived as teenagers, rates and total numbers. England and Wales 1971-1991**

a) Rates

b) Total numbers

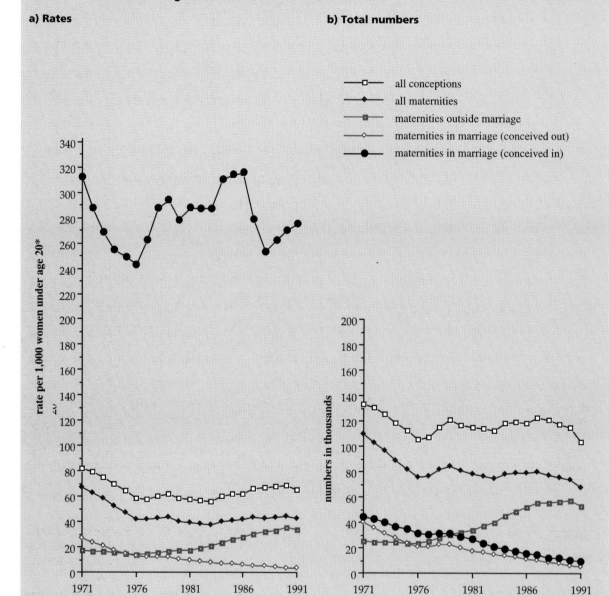

* The base populations are 'women under 20' for all conceptions and maternities; 'unmarried women under 20' for maternities outside marriage and maternities in marriage (conceived outside marriage) and 'married women under 20' for maternities in marriage (conceived inside).

Source: OPCS (1987) and (1994a).

BOX 1   continued

- The average age of a woman at first birth has increased by around two years over the period under study, from 24 in 1971 to 26 in 1991.[7]

- Increases in teen births over the 1980s were essentially about the behaviour of women aged 18 and 19. Their annual rate doubled during the decade and they accounted for 60 per cent of births to teenage women by 1992 (Figure 9). Those to women aged under 16 at conception, remained remarkably constant.

Figure 9   **Trends in out-of-marriage maternities for women conceiving under age twenty, by single ages (rates and total numbers). England and Wales 1971-1991**

a) Rates   b) Total numbers

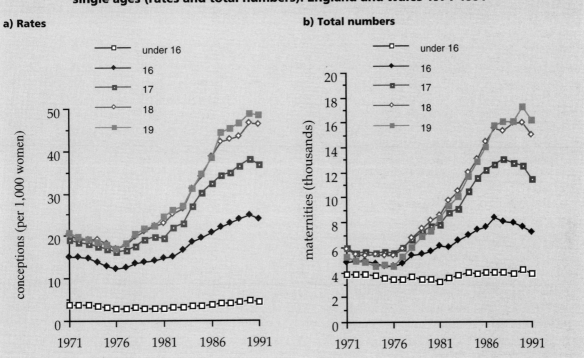

Source: OPCS (1987) and (1994a).

- Since 1988, the number of out-of-marriage maternities involving teenagers has been in decline. The out-of-marriage pregnancy rate (per thousand women) continued upwards until 1990 and has since declined.[8]

- Taken overall, the statistical evidence does not support the popular notion that we are in a period of unprecedented teenage sexual activity and childbearing, least of all where 'under age' mothers are concerned.

Never married motherhood and single lone motherhood

How does the flow of women into never-married motherhood, as so far described, relate to growth in the number of single lone mothers? Figure 10 illustrates the two main pathways:

A is the pathway taken by mothers who have never been married and who are not living with a partner at the time their babies are born.

B is the pathway followed by mothers who have never been married but who were cohabiting when their babies were born. Single lone parenthood is the result of a subsequent breakdown in that relationship.

Pathway A: births to lone mothers

Birth statistics give no definitive guide to whether a baby's mother was or was not residing with the father at the time of registration. The way the data is recorded can only lead to conjecture:

- Births registered by the mother alone may mean – but certainly do not prove – that a lone parent family has been formed directly. Since parents who are not married must both attend if they want a joint registration, or else provide a statutory declaration of paternity, it is likely that ignorance, apathy, lack of opportunity, or deliberate choice may result in some children whose parents are cohabiting being registered by their mothers alone.

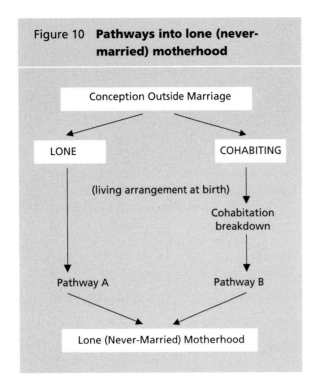

Figure 10 **Pathways into lone (never-married) motherhood**

Figure 11 **Estimates of births outside marriage, by form of registration. England and Wales 1971-1992.**

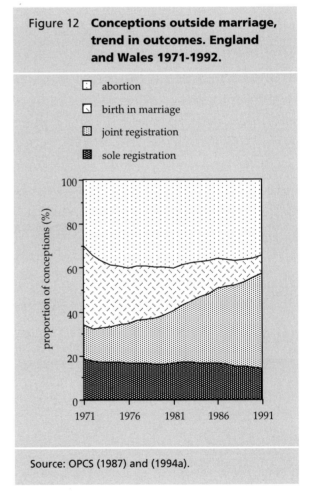

Source: OPCS (1987) and (1994a)

- Joint registration, although suggesting the mother's continued involvement with the father following the birth, does not necessarily point to cohabitation. However, one notable feature of recent births outside marriage births has been a marked increase in the proportion registered by both parents. In 1971 the majority of extra-marital births (55%) were registered by the mother alone, but by 1992 three quarters (76%) were registered jointly. Registration of births to women under 25 accounts for most of the overall change. By 1993 two thirds of such births to women under 20 were jointly registered as were more than three quarters to those between 20 and 24.[9]

Jointly registered births account for some 90 per cent of the recent increase in out-of-marriage births (Figure 11). Nevertheless, the absolute number of births registered by the mother alone rose from by nearly 20 thousand over the 1970s and 1980s (from 35 thousand in 1971 to a peak of 54.8 thousand in 1990) but has since been in decline (50.2 thousand in 1993).[10]

Figure 12, meanwhile, suggests that changing responses to pregnancies outside marriage have effectively brought about a transfer from births inside marriage (following 'shotgun' weddings) to the joint registration of births outside marriage.

Clearly not all of the out-of-marriage births described in Figure 11 were to single, never-married women. However, data on birth registration according to mother's age can be applied to the estimated age profile of births to never-married women to produce estimates of

Figure 12 **Conceptions outside marriage, trend in outcomes. England and Wales 1971-1992.**

☐ abortion

◹ birth in marriage

▦ joint registration

▦ sole registration

Source: OPCS (1987) and (1994a).

the way that births to never-married mothers are registered. The results are shown in Figure 13 which suggests that 74 per cent of births to never-married women in 1992 were jointly registered (compared with 76 per cent of all births outside marriage).

Single lone mothers: problems, prospects and policies

Figure 13	Estimates of births to never-married women by form of registration. England and Wales 1971-1991.

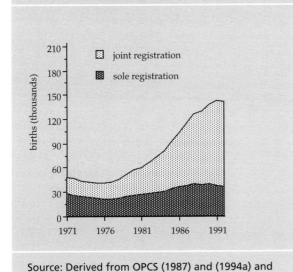

Source: Derived from OPCS (1987) and (1994a) and Cooper, J (1991).

Table 2 Jointly registered births outside marriage, percentage giving same or different addresses by age. England and Wales

age of mother	1983	1992
all ages	same 73.1	72.8
	diff 26.9	27.2
under 20	same 56.5	57.2
	diff 43.5	42.8
20-24	same 76.2	71.6
	diff 23.8	28.4
25-29	same 83.1	78.2
	diff 16.9	21.8
30-34	same 82.2	80.2
	diff 17.8	19.8
35 and over	same 80.0	79.7
	diff 20.0	20.3

Source: OPCS (1987) and (1994a).

'Same' and 'different address' registrations

Since 1983, joint registration statistics have taken note of whether a baby's parents give the same or separate addresses. Table 2 shows that the likelihood of a 'same address' registration increases with mothers age, from 57 per cent of joint registrations among the under 20's to 80 per cent where the mother is over 35

- In three out of four cases both partners give the same address, which is generally taken to mean that they are cohabiting.

- Joint registrations at different addresses are a more problematic category which in 1992 accounted for just over one in five out of marriage births. It will include, for example, couples who hope to cohabit or marry, but for a range of reasons – such as failure to attain or afford suitable accommodation – have not done so. (Such constraints may, indeed, account for the apparently lower cohabitation rate among young mothers). But it may also include parents who wished both their names to appear on the birth certificate even though they had no plans to cohabit

Even with the data concerning addresses, it is impossible to use registration statistics as a direct measure of the nature and strength of parental relationships. A conservative estimate might, nevertheless, be that during the past decade just

over half of all births outside marriage have been to cohabiting couples – and, consequently, that just under half were to women who, however briefly, were lone parents.

The specific focus for this pathway is, however, women who have never been married. Their younger age profile would seem to suggest that a lower proportion are likely to be living in cohabiting unions at the time of birth and that a somewhat higher proportion are lone parents. However, only a very broad, 'ballpark' estimate can be attempted since there may be factors other than age causing never-married mothers to register their births differently from other unmarried mothers. Any estimate also assumes that births jointly registered at the same address are to cohabiting parents. Nevertheless, taking these factors into account it would appear that between 40 and 50 per cent of never-married women who give birth outside marriage are cohabiting at the time.

Pathway B: Single lone motherhood as a result of cohabitation breakdown

Some never-married mothers become single, lone mothers at the moment their babies are born (Pathway A). But others, who were cohabiting at the time their babies were born, subsequently enter the statistics as a result of relationship breakdown. In order to estimate the contribution this latter train of events has made to the overall increase in single lone parenthood it is necessary to consider what is known about the extent of cohabitation among never-married mothers and the stability of those unions.

At the end of the analysis of 'Pathway A', it was suggested that probably more than 40 per cent of births to never-married women in recent years have been to cohabiting couples.[11] An analysis of the OPCS Longitudinal Study[12] by Audrey Brown has provided some further evidence on cohabitation breakdown.[13] Using joint registration as a proxy for cohabitation the study attempted to measure the stability of such unions during the 1970s.[14] The analysis suggests that cohabitation at the birth of a baby may often be of fairly temporary duration. Of children jointly registered at birth, just over a fifth were estimated still to be in cohabiting couple families by the time of the 1981 Census. The most common outcome – for half the (assumed) cohabiting couples – was marriage, but more than a quarter of the relationships had broken down into single lone parenthood.

More recent research by Susan McRae supports the view that marriage is the most common outcome for women who are cohabiting when their children are born.[15] Of 166 such mothers,[16] less than half were still cohabiting 4 years after a birth; a third were married and one in five had separated and become single lone mothers. However, an analysis by John Ermisch of life histories collected in the British Household Panel Study, estimates that roughly as many never-married women who have children while cohabiting can expect to become never-married mothers as will marry – just over four out of ten within 10 years of the birth. He suggests that cohabitation involving younger women -like marriages – may be at greater risk of breakdown.[17]

A 1989 national survey of lone parents by Jonathan Bradshaw and Jane Millar, meanwhile, found that most single lone mothers had been without a resident partner when their baby was born (Figure 14). The remaining 16 per cent had been in cohabitations that had broken down at some time after the birth.[18]

This figure for the proportion of single lone mothers who had been cohabiting when their babies were born may seem low. It must be remembered, however, that the popularity of cohabitation has increased very rapidly in recent years. The mothers surveyed by Bradshaw and Millar (Figure 14) included women who had become lone parents at a time when cohabitation was less common than now. Given the greater

Figure 14	Routes into single lone motherhood
Living arrangement prior to birth – (percentages)	
Living with parents	58%
Living Alone	17%
Living with Relatives	9%
Cohabiting	16%

Source: Bradshaw, J. and Millar, J. (1991).

proportion of births to never-married mothers in the early 1990s that this analysis attributes to cohabiting couples, it is to be expected that cohabitation breakdown is responsible for a higher proportion than formerly of the influx to single lone motherhood. Moreover, as cohabitation among never-married mothers increases at the expense of marriage, so too does the likelihood that women who would once have entered the lone parent statistics as separated or divorced will nowadays do so as single lone mothers.

Commentary

The limited evidence that can be extracted from birth statistics and elsewhere suggests that in the last twenty years teenage women have accounted for a declining proportion of all out-of-marriage births and that the average age at which women first give birth is continuing to rise (Box 1). The rate and absolute number of births to unmarried teenagers did increase fairly consistently from the late 1970s to the early 1990s, but an increasing proportion were registered by both parents. There is, therefore, little evidence of any major increase in births to unattached teenage women. It is, however, very likely that a growing proportion of single lone mothers are women who have experienced the breakdown in their cohabiting relationship.

In the light of these findings there are two assumptions commonly made in debates about the rise of single lone motherhood that will have to be tempered.

• It is incorrect to assume that the increase is simply the consequence of a rise in out-of-marriage births among young women.

• It is a mistake to suppose that the women who become single lone parents have done so without attempting or hoping to establish a cohabiting partnership with the father.

Decline of the shotgun marriage

The increase in single lone motherhood may be closely related to the rapid decline in the number of 'shotgun' weddings. For where pregnancy might once have prompted young couples to get married before their baby was born, it is now more likely to lead to cohabitation.[19] And just as 'shotgun' marriages are less stable than other marriages,[20] so there is evidence of considerable degree of instability in the cohabitations formed by today's young mothers-to-be (see above). But while the breakdown of a 'shotgun' marriage increases the numbers of separated or divorced lone parents, the breakdown of an equivalent cohabitation with children swells the ranks of single lone parenthood.(Figure 15). One consequence of the decline of the shotgun wedding may, therefore, have been to effect a net shift of women from one lone parent category to another.

Figure 16 below gives some indication of the number of 'extra' out-of-marriage maternities that might have occurred in different age groups as a result of the decline in shotgun weddings. The estimates assume that the ratio of maternities inside to those outside marriage (resulting from conceptions outside marriage) observed in 1971 had held constant to 1991.[21] The proportion of abortions is left unmodified. This calculation suggests that the decline in the shotgun wedding since 1971 may have resulted in more than 550 thousand extra maternities to the never-married (whether single lone or cohabiting) over 20 years. It is noticeable that these fall almost entirely into the younger age groups, reflecting the fact that during the years of their greatest popularity, most shotgun weddings involved women under 25.

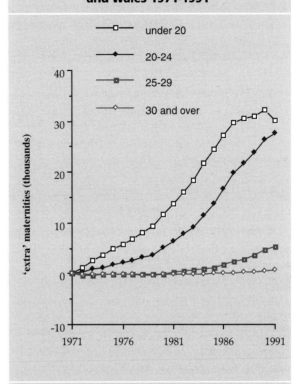

Figure 16   Estimated number of 'extra' maternities to never-married women by age, resulting from the decreasing share of out-of-marriage conceptions becoming in-marriage maternities. England and Wales 1971-1991*

* Based on the assumption that the proportion of maternities (from out-of- marriage conceptions) that fell within marriage had held constant at the 1971 level.

Source: Estimated from OPCS (1987) and (1994a) and Cooper, J. (1991).

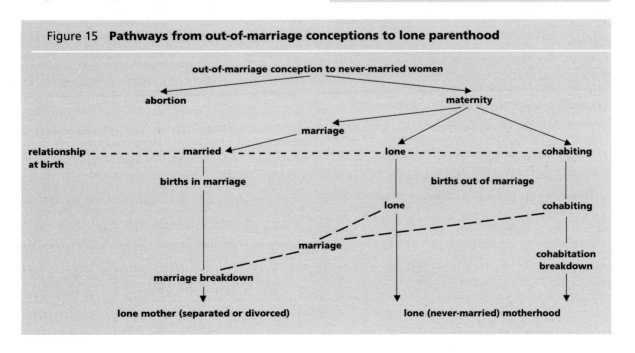

Figure 15   Pathways from out-of-marriage conceptions to lone parenthood

Effect on lone parenthood

Further speculation as to the difference these trends has made to the numbers of lone parents by separation or divorce relative to the number of single lone mothers is difficult. Such a calculation would require estimates for the level of relationship breakdown among shotgun marriages and cohabiting couples with children. Flows out of lone parenthood would also need to be taken into account.

Existing research does, however, indicate that breakdown rates for shotgun marriages are higher than average. Kathleen Kiernan, for example, found that one in four marriages of teenage brides who conceived before marriage had broken down by the time the women were 32.[22] And John Haskey, using divorce rates for 1980-1, has estimated that as many as one in two teenage brides will eventually divorce.[23]

If the assumptions in Figure 16 are an adequate reflection of trends, it is reasonable to suppose that current levels of lone parenthood through separation or divorce would be significantly higher now had shotgun weddings retained their popularity. Conversely, the numbers of single lone mothers would be significantly lower. As matters stand, a further increase in the number of cohabitations involving never-married mothers can be expected to add to the numbers of single lone parents when relationships break down.

Informing the demographic debate

As this chapter has shown, the limited statistical sources which provide information on an individual's cohabitation history do not make it possible to disaggregate accurately the growth in single lone mothers by route of entry. There is, however, enough indirect evidence to suggest that the rise in cohabitation and the growth in single lone motherhood are causally linked. This, in turn, indicates that the existing system of lone parent categorisation is failing to provide an accurate picture of the dynamics of family formation and lone parenthood.

If existing limitations to the analysis of the formation and dissolution of families are to be resolved, cohabitation histories will increasingly be needed. But there is also a strong case for making fundamental changes to the classification of lone parent groups. In particular the increasing numeric importance of 'cohabitation breakdown' as a route to lone parenthood needs to be distinguished within the collection and presentation of statistics.

Notes

1   For ease of presentation, 'single lone (never-married) mothers' are referred to in the report as 'single lone mothers'. A longer version of this chapter will appear in the FPSC working paper series.

2   Increased rates but a declining share of the total number of conceptions reflect the shrinking cohorts of younger women. There have been, in other words, fewer unmarried teenagers to become pregnant. At the same time, the older cohorts have got larger just as their out of marriage conception rates increased.

3   Birth statistics for 1993 are now available. They confirm the direction of recent trends, notably the tentative signs of a decline in out-of-marriage births among teenage women. Women aged over 30 continue to show the greatest proportional increase in out-of-marriage births. However, provisional data for 1994 indicate, after 20 years of increase, a levelling off in the proportion of all births that are outside marriage (Babb and Bethune, 1995).

4   Cooper, J. (1991).

5   Babb, P (1993).

6   While this does mask some increase from the 1983 trough of 37.3 per thousand, the trend since 1990 has been downward (OPCS, 995a).

7   OPCS (1987) and (1995).

8   Babb and Betune (1995) and OPCS (1955a).

9   OPCS (1995c).

10 OPCS (1995c).

11 This figure is higher than that suggested by Kiernan, K. & Estaugh, V. (1993) whose analysis of 1989 GHS data found that 3 out of 10 never-married mothers were cohabiting The discrepancy may indicate one or a combination of three things: 1) that the assumptions linking joint registration with cohabitation are inaccurate, 2) that cohabitations existing at the birth of a baby to a never-married women are liable to be short lived, resulting either in marriage or breakdown into single lone motherhood, or 3) that the differences reflect problems of comparisons of 'flows' (births) with 'stocks' (lone mothers) that have been built up over a long time. Kiernan and Estaugh's sample included women with dependent children up to 16 years old whose family circumstances could well have changed between birth registration and General Household Survey interview.

12 Based on a sub-sample of the national Census.

13 Brown, A. (1986).

14 This was a difficult exercise because the 1981 Census did not recognise 'cohabitation' as a formal category in the family classifications and cohabiting couples with dependent children were misleadingly grouped in with lone parent families. Cohabitations could be reconstructed indirectly from the Census data where a 'de facto spouse' was recorded, but, as the author recognised, there was a risk of overstating the flow of children of cohabiting couples into lone parent families.

15 McRae, S. (1993).

16 Not all of the mothers were 'never-married' women.

17 Ermisch, J. (forthcoming).

18 Bradshaw, J. and Millar, J. (1991).

19 As shown earlier in this chapter, more than half of maternities resulting from out of marriage conceptions occurred in marriage in 1971, and were thus earmarked for this pathway. In 1991 it had fallen to just 9%, resulting in a massive increase in the proportion and number of maternities occurring outside marriage.

20 They are more likely to do so, particularly among for younger women, than those where conceptions take place after a marriage. (Kiernan, K.E. 1986).

21 By 1991, the proportion of extra-marital conceptions leading to marriage before maternity had, in fact, fallen to 13 per cent.

22 Kiernan, K.E. (1986).

23 Haskey, J. (1986).

Single lone mothers: problems, prospects and policies

Social and economic characteristics

3

In this chapter, data from the General Household Survey (GHS) is used to explore the social and economic circumstances of single lone mothers with dependent[1] children. Comparisons are not only made between family types – single lone, other lone, cohabiting and married couples – but also within the focus group of single lone mother families.

To create a healthy sample size, data from three years of the survey, 1990-1992, was combined[2] (Table 1). Within the single lone mother category, however, it was not possible to distinguish between women who had previously cohabited and those who had always lived alone.

Table 1	Number and percentage of families with dependent children, 1990-1992			
	Single lone mother	Other lone mother	Cohabiting couples	Married couples	Total
	613	1076	492	6947	9128
	6.7%	11.8%	5.4%	76.1%	100%

Source: General Household Survey, 1990-1992.

Families and households

Table 2 shows that single lone mother families are distinguished from other families by the relatively high proportion (one in five), living with their own parents.

Table 2	Proportion of families living alone or with others, 1990-1992			
	Single lone mother %	Other lone mother %	Cohabiting couples %	Married couples %
Family alone	75.9	90.8	95.1	95.8
With parents	20.9	6.1	1.6	3.1
With others	3.3	3.1	3.3	1.1

Source: General Household Survey, 1990-1992.

Age of mother

Only a very small proportion of single lone mothers – less than one in 10 – are under 20 years old (Table 3). They do, however, have a younger age profile; just over a half are over 25 years compared with at least three-quarters of other mothers whether cohabiting, married, separated, divorced or widowed.

Table 3	Current age of mother – proportions by age group, 1990-1992			
	Single lone mother %	Other lone mother %	Cohabiting couples %	Married couples %
Up to 20	8.6	.3	2.8	.2
20-24	37.4	4.5	21.3	4.5
25 and over	54.0	95.3	75.8	95.3

Source: General Household Survey, 1990-1992.

Moreover, just under half the single lone mothers were aged under 20 when their first child was born. This was less likely to be the case for other mothers, although three out of 10 cohabiting and other lone mothers also had a first child during their teens. Conversely, single lone mothers were much less likely than married mothers to have been 25 years or older when they had their first child – only one in seven compared with almost a half (Table 4).

Table 4	Age of mother at birth of first child – proportions by age group, 1990-1992			
	Single lone mother %	Other lone mother %	Cohabiting couples %	Married couples %
Up to 20	47.0	30.3	32.3	14.3
20-24	38.8	40.3	41.6	37.9
25 and over	14.2	29.3	26.2	47.8

Source: General Household Survey, 1990-1992.

Children

Single lone mothers have younger and fewer children than other families (Tables 5 and 6). Seven out of 10 single lone mothers have only one child and most of these are under five. Very few single lone mothers have a youngest child as old as 10.

Table 5	Dependent children by family type, 1990-1992			
	Single lone mother %	Other lone mother %	Cohabiting couples %	Married couples %
One child	70.1	41.1	52.8	37.6
Two or more	29.9	58.9	47.2	62.4

Source: General Household Survey, 1990-1992.

Table 6	Age of youngest dependent child by family type, 1990-1992			
	Single lone mother %	Other lone mother %	Cohabiting couples %	Married couples %
0-4	71.3	31.7	61.8	41.8
5-9	21.0	28.8	19.5	24.3
10-18	7.7	39.5	18.7	33.9

Source: General Household Survey, 1990-1992.

Housing

Three-quarters of single lone mothers live in rented accommodation and barely one in five are owner occupiers (Table 7). This is in marked contrast to all other families with dependent children. Indeed, the housing circumstances of single lone mothers and married parents are reverse images of each other with more than three out of four living in rented accommodation and in owner-occupied homes respectively. Even all other lone mothers are more than twice as likely to own their own homes.

Even so, these figures overestimate the true level of owner occupation among single lone mothers. This is partly because the headline count includes some women who are living with their own parents. When analysed separately (Table 14), the extent of owner occupation among single lone mothers falls – although it still appears high compared with previous estimates.[3]

Table 7	Housing tenure: proportions by family type, 1990-1992			
	Single lone mother %	Other lone mother %	Cohabiting couples %	Married couples %
Owner occupier	19.4	43.0	48.0	78.5
Rented – LA or HA*	72.8	50.8	42.2	16.2
Other rented	7.8	6.1	9.8	5.3

* Local authority or housing association.

Source: General Household Survey, 1990-1992.

Income and economic activity

Between 1990 and 1992, more than three out of four single lone mother families had a net weekly income of less than £100 a week compared with four out of 10 in other lone parent families. Couple families, by comparison, were most unlikely to have such a low net income.

Table 8	Net weekly income of parents by family type, 1990-1992			
	Single lone mother %	Other lone mother %	Cohabiting couples %	Married couples %
Up to £99	76.2	45.8	13.4	5.3
£100 or more	23.8	54.2	86.7	94.7
	£	£	£	£
Average (mean)	88.9	129.2	244.1	322.6

Note: Income is net of tax and national insurance.

Source: General Household Survey, 1990-1992.

Over eight out of 10 single lone mothers were receiving Income Support compared with six out of 10 other lone mothers. The GHS data, meanwhile, confirms the findings of other surveys that receipt of child maintenance from 'absent' fathers is low for all lone parent families and particularly so for single lone mothers.[4] Only one in six single lone mothers was receiving maintenance, as were just over a third of other lone mothers.

Paid work is a major determinant of family

income – and single lone mothers were markedly less likely to have jobs than other mothers with dependent children. A higher proportion were, however, looking for work (Table 9).

Table 9	Economic activity of mothers, 1990-1992			
	Single lone mother %	Other lone mother %	Cohabiting couples %	Married couples %
Working	28.7	49.1	53.7	63.5
Seeking work	7.5	5.1	5.7	3.0
Keeping house	60.5	40.4	38.8	31.7
Other/inactive	3.3	5.3	1.8	1.8

Source: General Household Survey, 1990-1992.

This pattern of working and keeping house accords with findings from other surveys, reflecting, in part, the higher proportion of single lone mothers with children under five. The minority of single lone mothers who were working between 1990-2 had average net weekly earnings that were around 15 per cent lower than those of other mothers. There was no comparable difference between the average earnings of other lone, cohabiting and married mothers (Table 10).

Table 10	Current average net weekly earnings for mothers and couples, 1990-1992	
	mothers £	couples £
Single lone mother	87.4	–
Other lone mothers	102.0	–
Cohabiting couple	105.2	266.3
Married couple	100.1	320.8

Source: General Household Survey, 1990-1992.

Furthermore, by separating the earnings of mothers from those of their partners (the difference between the columns in Table 10), it is evident how much difference the contribution of husbands and partners make to the gross incomes of two-parent families.

Among the minority of single lone mothers who had paid jobs, a larger proportion were employed part-time (less than 16 hours a week) than among other mothers. Nonetheless, almost two-thirds of single lone mothers in employment were working full-time (more than 16 hours a

week) and four out of 10 were working more than thirty hours a week.

Table 11	Hours of work, 1990-1992			
Hours per week	Single lone mother %	Other lone mother %	Cohabiting couples %	Married couples %
1-15	35.6	27.1	19.7	28.5
16-29	20.3	28.8	29.0	33.9
30 or more	44.1	44.0	51.4	37.6
Total	100.0	100.0	100.0	100.0

Source: General Household Survey, 1990-1992.

This overall pattern of economic activity is likely to reflect not only the pre-school age profile of their children, but also the cost of child care relative to their potential or actual earnings. It is, however, instructive to compare single lone mothers' working patterns with those of cohabiting mothers – who are only slightly less likely to be caring for a child under five. Despite this, half the cohabiting mothers in employment were working more than 30 hours a week.

Meanwhile, more than a third of single lone mothers who were working full-time were receiving Family Credit – as were a fifth of the other lone mothers.

Educational qualifications

Almost four out of 10 single lone mothers in the General Household Survey had no educational qualifications, although in this they did not differ significantly from other lone parents. Fewer cohabiting and married were at the same disadvantage. Single lone mothers were also less likely to have higher educational qualifications. Only one in 10 had 'A' levels or a degree compared with more than a quarter of married mothers.

Table 12	Highest education qualification, 1990-1992			
	Single lone mother %	Other lone mother %	Cohabiting couples %	Married couples %
None	37.8	39.8	31.7	29.6
GCSE*	51.4	42.4	51.2	43.4
A level*	4.5	6.0	7.5	8.1
Degree or above	6.2	11.8	9.6	18.9

* And equivalent level qualifications.

Source: General Household Survey, 1990-1992.

Characteristics by age

The different social and economic characteristics of single lone mother families can be analysed according to the mother's age (Table 13).[5] This underlines the dominance of very young children over the working lives of younger single lone mothers. The proportion of single lone mothers in paid work doubles between the youngest and oldest age groups and hours of work steadily increase.[6]

Hand in hand with this goes the overwhelming financial dependence of younger mothers (under 25) on Income Support. For all but a very few in 1990-2, net weekly incomes were less than £100. Only among those aged 25 years and above could a larger minority of mothers be found with incomes over £100. Even then, eight out of 10 of these older mothers were receiving Income Support.

The patterns of housing tenure were less clear cut. Owner occupation was highest among the youngest mothers, but mainly (the figures in Table 14 suggest) because they were living with their parents. Single lone mothers were most unlikely to be in owner-occupied accommodation when they were living independently and rental accommodation predominated for those not living with their parents.

Living 'at home' or alone

Further comparisons between single lone mothers living independently and those living with their parents (Table 14) reveal that the latter were more likely to have a child under five years old. It might also have been anticipated that those living with parents would be more likely to take paid work – given the possible availability of grandparents as carers. In fact, the proportions of single lone mothers in employment were low in both cases – although a substantially higher proportion of those living with parents who *did* have jobs worked for more than 30 hours a week.

Table 13   **Characteristics of single lone mothers and their children by age group of mother, 1990-1992**

		Age of mother		
		Up to 20	**20-24**	**25 and over**
Number of mothers in sample:		53	229	331
		%	%	%
Age of youngest dependent child:	0-4	100	92.1	52.3
	5-9	–	7.0	34.1
	10-18	–	0.9	13.6
Housing tenure:	owner-occupier	22.6	18.8	19.3
	rented LA/HA[1]	64.2	71.2	75.2
Weekly income:[2]	under £50	16.7	4.7	3.5
	£50-£100	79.2	82.8	62.1
	£100 or more	4.2	12.6	34.4
Receiving Income Support		95.7	89.0	81.6
Receiving maintenance		10.4	17.3	15.7
In paid employment:		15.0	20.1	36.6
Hours or work:	1-15	75.0	43.8	29.8
	16-29	0.0	20.8	21.5
	30 or more	25.0	35.4	48.8

1. Local authority or housing association.

2. Current income net of tax and national insurance.

Source: General Household Survey, 1990-1992.

Table 14 Characteristics of single lone mothers and their children by whether living with mother's parents, 1990-1992

		Living with parents	Living independently
Number of mothers in sample:		128	485
		%	%
Age of youngest dependent child:	0-4	79.7	69.1
	5-9	15.6	22.5
	10-18	4.7	8.5
Housing tenure:	owner-occupier	53.1	10.5
	rented LA/HA[1]	43.0	80.6
Weekly income[2]:	under £50	9.7	3.9
	£50-£100	68.1	71.9
	£100 or more	22.1	24.2
Receiving Income Support		80.9	86.7
Receiving maintenance		13.7	16.4
In paid employment:		29.0	28.0
Hours or work:	1-15	16.2	40.7
	16-29	18.9	20.7
	30 or more	64.9	38.6

1. Local authority or housing association.

2. Current income net of tax and national insurance.

Source: General Household Survey, 1990-1992.

Notes

1 Children up to the age of 16; or 19 if they are in full-time education.

2 We are extremely grateful to Charlie Owen at the Thomas Coram Research Unit who carried out this analysis for us.

3 For example, Bradshaw, J. and Millar, J. (1991).

4 Burghes, L. (1993).

5 The small number of single mothers under 20 in the GHS sample means that some of the findings should be treated with caution.

6 The small sample size seems to be a particular problem for the employment figures for the youngest age group of mothers for whom there were probably less than 10 in paid employment.

Part II
The Qualitative Study

The research

Previous studies have explored the circumstances in which teenagers become pregnant and then give birth. The events and influences that determine whether a young mother is single, cohabiting or married when her baby is born have received less attention. The aim of the qualitative research conducted for this study was to shed new light on the pathways that take young women from their early sexual experiences and conception to single lone motherhood. Put another way, 'how did they get where they are today, and why?'.

Background

Teenage fertility in Britain, unlike other European countries, underwent an increase in the 1980s – although it has recently begun to decline.[1] Explanations for this have, among other areas, been sought in the field of sex education and young people's knowledge and use of contraception. Yet research suggests that knowledge of contraception among teenagers has become so widespread that ignorance alone cannot account for the trend.[2] This is notwithstanding the fact that myths about unprotected sex continue to circulate[3] and that some teenagers feel that sex education remains inadequate.[4]

Recent studies emphasise two other underlying factors. Firstly, that the majority of sexually active teenagers will not be trying to conceive – even if a small minority are.[5] Secondly, that theoretical understanding of family planning methods is not sufficient on its own to ensure that teenagers have access to contraception and use it. Teenagers under 16 years are, for example, not automatically entitled to contraceptive advice.[6] The nature of developing relationships between young teenage girls and boys may also make it difficult for them to take contraceptive precautions before sexual intercourse occurs. Although more than a third of teenage copnceptions are terminated,[7] not all young women approve of abortion and some find the prospect unsettling.

Teenage births

For those teenage conceptions that do lead to maternity the most notable change of the past 25 years has been the increased likelihood of their taking place outside marriage.[8] As already seen, these extra-marital births include a growing proportion where the parents are cohabiting, as well as births to single lone mothers. But what are the underlying factors? To what extent are the outcomes for individual teenagers influenced by their own attitudes and those of their families and friends? What part do income, availability of housing and other practical considerations play? Is the increase in single lone motherhood a consequence of positive choices or of hopes that have been dashed? These are some of the questions which the qualitative survey was intended to address.

Research design

The mothers

The study focused on teenage women who had been 'at risk', as teenagers, of single lone motherhood. Risk was, in this instance, defined as having been unmarried when they conceived or when they engaged in sexual activity.[9] A total of 31 mothers were interviewed, of whom 19 were single lone mothers and 12 were cohabiting or married. Mothers aged under 16 year were not included in the research.[10] However, a third group, of eight teenage girls, who were childless, but sexually active, was also interviewed.

- The **single lone mothers** in the survey were all living alone with their dependent children and had never been married. All had given birth to their first baby within the last five years.

- The **cohabiting mothers,** whose first babies were also born within the previous five years, were living now with a male partner – though not always the father of their first child.

Defining the comparative groups of women in this way allowed an exploration of the landmark stages of conception, birth and family status.[11] However, the terms 'single' and 'cohabiting' should not be taken to mean more than they do. Some of the single lone mothers were in relationships, although not cohabiting. Nor were those single lone mother without a current partner necessarily raising their children alone; support was often available from family and friends.

Family change

Since the intention was to explore the dynamic nature of single lone motherhood, a positive decision was taken to include the mothers of toddlers under five as well as those who had recently given birth. This longer time-scale made it possible to include women who were now cohabiting, but who had been single lone mothers when their babies were born. Interviewing some mothers a number of years after the birth also avoided catching them all in a post-natal phase when life might seem abnormally rosy or bleak.

Demographic, social and economic characteristics

The survey aimed to achieve a mix of demographic, social and economic characteristics among the young women. A balance was sought between

- Women who were 'younger' teenagers of 16 and 17 when they first gave birth and those who were 'older' teenagers.

- Mothers living with their parents and those living independently.

- Mothers with children aged under two and those with children between two and four years.

Efforts were also taken to include a range of socio-economic backgrounds (according to their parents' occupations since few mothers were employed themselves). Some variation in housing tenure and residence in a mix of urban and rural areas was also sought.

The sample characteristics

Recruitment proved difficult due to the understandable reluctance of some young mothers to disclose personal and family details. As a result, the selected sample did not exactly match the detailed quotas we had devised. It did, however, capture most of the range of the characteristics. It proved particularly hard to find

young mothers living with partners, mothers in employment and living in anything other than rented accommodation. On the other hand, this was not unexpected in the light of national survey data. 'Younger' cohabiting mothers with young children were a difficult group to recruit. It is possible that this reflected the practical barriers preventing 16 and 17 year olds from obtaining independent housing . Many mothers (chapter 7) reported not being allowed to put their names on the local authority housing waiting list until they were 18.

In the end, slightly more interviews than planned were undertaken – 39 rather than 36 (Box 1). Fewer cohabiting mothers were found than had been hoped (12 compared with 14) and more single mothers were recruited as result (19 compared with the 14 planned).

Box 1	Number of mothers and young women interviewed
Single mothers	19*
Cohabiting mothers	12
Teenage women	8*
Total	39
* one of each interview produced very little usable data.	

More 18 and 19 year old women were interviewed than originally intended (Box 2). However, half the single lone mothers and the majority of the cohabiting mothers had their first child at 17 or 18 years.

Box 2	Age of mothers at birth of first child				
	16	17	18	19	Total
Single mothers	3	3	8	5	19
Cohabiting mothers	1	5	5	1	12
Total	4	8	13	6	31

Boxes 3 and 4 demonstrate that there was a bigger age difference between single and cohabiting mothers (and those of their children) at the time of interview than there was between their ages at the time of first birth.

Box 3	Age of mothers and young women at interview			
	Single mothers	Cohabiting mothers	Teenage women	Total
16	-	-	3	3
17	2	-	3	5
18	2	1	1	4
19	4	-	1	5
20	2	3	-	5
21	5	2	-	7
22	1	3	-	4
23	3	3	-	6
Total	19	12	8	39

Box 4	Age of first child at mother's interview		
Ages of children	Single mothers	Cohabiting mothers	Total
under 6 mths	1	-	1
6 mth – 1 yr*	3	-	3
1 yr – 2 yrs	7	2	9
2 yrs – 3 yrs	1	2	3
3 yrs – 4 yrs	2	3	5
4 yrs plus	5	5	10
0 – 2 years	11	2	13
2 years plus	8	10	18
Total	19	12	31

* this should be read as 'under 1 year' and likewise for each of the following age groupings.

No quotas were set for second children. Information on family size at the time of interview is shown in Box 5. Given their older age profile, it is not surprising that cohabiting mothers were more likely to have second children.

Box 5	Number of mothers with second and subsequent children		
	Second child	Second and third child	Total
Single mothers	3	2	5 (of 19)
Cohabiting mothers	7	-	7 (of 12)
Total	10	2	12

Box 6 shows there was some disparity in the socio-economic profiles of the single lone and the cohabiting mothers.

Box 6	Social class of mothers based on their father's occupation						
	A	B	C1	C2	D	E	Total*
Single mothers	-	2	3	5	6	1	17
Cohabiting mothers	-	-	1	5	4	-	10
Teenage women	-	2	0	4	1	-	7
Total	-	4	4	14	11	1	34

Note: * A social class could not be assigned for two of the single and two of the cohabiting mothers and for one of the teenage women.

Reporting the findings

The mothers talked freely to the interviewers about the experience of single motherhood. Their verbatim comments, reported in the chapters that follow, often portray their feelings and attitudes in a vivid way that analysis and interpretation could not necessarily achieve.[12] It needs to be understood, however, that this was 'qualitative', not 'quantitative' research. The interviews were carried out in a depth not possible in larger surveys; but the numbers of mothers interviewed (at 31) was small and not necessarily representative of the single lone mother population as a whole. It should also be noted that no information was collected directly from male partners. It is, therefore, the mothers' perceptions and memories of the fathers of their children that are reported.

Notes

1 See Box 1, chapter 2.

2 Phoenix, A. (1991).

3 Hudson, F. and Ineichen, B. (1991).

4 Allen, I. (1991).

5 See, for example, Simms, M. and Smith, C. (1986), Hudson, F. and Ineichen, B. (1991) and Phoenix, A. (1991).

6 Family Policy Studies Centre (1994).

7 See Chapter 2.

8 See Chapter 2.

9 A comparison with those not 'at risk' because they were already married was beyond the scope of this study.

10 There was a danger that the special circumstances of this statistically small group of mothers below the legal age of consent would have muddied the waters.

11 A more detailed description of the criteria for the comparison groups can be found in Appendix 1.

12 Quotations in the report are marked by an identifier code as follows: [1] for the single lone mothers; [2] for mothers in cohabiting relationships and [3] for teenage women.

5 Sexual experience and conception

This chapter is about how the young mothers in the survey came to be pregnant. It describes their perceptions of whatever education they received concerning sex, personal relationships and family life. It goes on to consider their sexual activity as teenagers, their knowledge and use of contraception and whether their pregnancies were planned.

Sex education and information

Most of the mothers interviewed could remember little about their formal sex education. Indeed nine out of the 19 single lone mothers insisted that they could not remember receiving any sex education at all:

"It wasn't really a lot ... it was a bit too quick ... you only get one lesson and it doesn't all drill into you ... I didn't understand it." [2]

"The only lessons that I can remember was when they were talking about periods." [2]

Those who could recall lessons in school said they often consisted of videos and explanatory leaflets. The most frequent complaint was that there was too little detail, too little explanation and no discussion. Only a few women considered their sex education had been good:

"I knew about the dangers ... about different diseases ... types of contraception ... I suppose that they did teach us everything that we needed to know." [1]

The best lessons were considered to be those that allowed potentially embarrassing questions to be answered and a frank discussion to take place.

"We all ... could write questions on a piece of paper ... and he'd put 'em all in a box and then he'd answer 'em. But he didn't know who were asking what questions, so that were good doing that ... you could ask questions what you wanted and like not feel embarrassed." [1]

Just a few said their own parents had been open and approachable, providing them with information or answering their questions about sex.

"If I asked she told me everything I needed to know." [1]

One woman said her mother had told her 'the facts of life' when she was 10:

"When I started having my periods ... any questions I asked she answered as best she could ... I certainly can't use the excuse that I didn't know." [1]

It was more common, however, for the mothers to report the opposite:

" ... in our house it was taboo, you don't say things like that." [2]

Two, however, identified alternative sources of information within their families:

"I always go to my auntie's for anything like that. I just feel awkward talking to my Mum. And they always answer my questions. She got me some leaflets from the Doctor's." [2]

Much information about sex, as distinct from education, was learned in the playground from friends. This may explain why some had paid scant attention to their sex education in school, believing by then that they 'knew all about it'. Gaps and inaccuracies in their understanding, consequently, went uncorrected:

"I found out more off my friends. But they normally tell it wrong and so I didn't really find out all of it." [2]

It was evident in the case of a few mothers that they had simply missed whatever sex education was on offer. Either it took place in lessons not attended by all pupils or else on days when the women were not in school. But being present during lessons was no guarantee that they would benefit from them. Many mothers remembered them as embarrassing occasions when the frequent response of pupils was to 'joke and muck about':

"... it was one big laugh really ... they put the boys in with the girls. I think that's where they went wrong ... everyone was giggling so I don't think anyone took it seriously." [2]

Some mothers also took the view that their age and general demeanour had meant they were unreceptive:

"I was at that age when I never listened to anybody." [1]

Others felt that their education had come either too early, or else too late. Those who made a case for earlier education thought younger children would be less embarrassed and more interested and attentive. They were concerned that sex education for some children was taking place so late that it followed rather than preceded sexual initiation:

"I think at 15 your too old 'cos some lassie's ... at 13 they're getting pregnant ... it should be done from a lot younger." [2]

Those opposed to early sex education argued that young people might find it irrelevant or fail to understand it:

" ... we was all young and we wasn't thinking of having babies." [2]

Not surprisingly, the childless but sexually active teenagers who were interviewed had a clearer recollection of their (relatively recent) sex education. This did not necessarily mean that what they had been taught was qualitatively better, but they were generally more positive about the experience and its importance:

"I've been lucky, both schools ... dealt with sex education in quite a lot of detail ... I think I'm pretty well informed – I seem to know about most things. I knew all about AIDS, all about STDs." [3]

But there were still those whose perception was that school sex education had been patchy. One teenager reported that her school did not provide sex education as a matter of principle.

Education about relationships and family life

Education about relationships and family life appeared to have been all but non-existent. Just a few of the childless teenagers could recall relevant school sessions. Overwhelmingly, however, it was something the mothers wished had been available:

"I think they should talk to you about all different kinds of things ... of young people of our age coping with a baby." [1]

They spoke about their ignorance of the realities of single lone motherhood and their wish that they had been better informed. A number raised the possibility that this might have averted their own early motherhood, especially if there had been an opportunity to talk to a teenage mother about her way of life:

" ... if she'd told us how it was it would have helped, but no one ever came in ... how much money it would be and how much care it would need. I don't think I would have had one." [1]

Some, however, did recall watching videos about teenage pregnancy which they had found off-putting at the time. One mother gave a particularly graphic account:

"When they showed you the video it put a lot of people off having babies ... the baby screaming all the time and nobody there to help her ... not getting much sleep at night and just generally wearing her down ... She had got a boyfriend but whenever she needed him he wasn't there ... when he did come in he was drunk ... so that didn't help her any ... a lot of people asked a lot of questions ... why she didn't take more care, why did she get pregnant." [2]

Sexual activity

Most of the single and the cohabiting mothers had their first experience of sexual intercourse at or just below the legal minimum age. All but a few were between 15 and 17 and at least half of both groups of mothers had conceived within a year of first intercourse.

The mothers spoke of a variety of influences that had precipitated their first sexual experience. Half the single lone mothers, but only two of the cohabiting mothers, had felt pressured into first intercourse. But the pressure to conform appeared at least as likely to have come from female peers as from boyfriends – although the two were by no means mutually exclusive:

"I think it were because all my friends had done it ... they were calling me a freak ... so I thought I'll have to do it so I wouldn't have anyone picking on me ... (he was) trying to make me go with him ... he said I was a lesbian and things like that." [1]

"I felt I had to ... He said, if you love someone and you are going out with them then you have got to have sex with them. I believed him at the time." [1]

Two of the single lone mothers described how they had resisted the pressure:

"I didn't believe them ... I didn't listen to them. In the end I was sick of them so I just told them I had." [1]

" ... there was all that, 'oh haven't you done it yet' ... it used to make me think what am I missing out on, but never actually made me do it." [1]

The cohabiting mothers were less likely to report peer pressure of this kind:

"I was with a group who just joked about it and mucked about at school. Never did it or anything ... me Mum and Dad put you off a little bit ... they told us what was right and wrong." [2]

"I said no, kept on saying no virtually, I just wanted him to want me for me." [2]

"I used to think it were disgusting at that age at school. I didn't like it ... I used to walk off. I didn't want to know. I knew legal age was 16 and I don't think they should do it until they're allowed to do it." [2]

Seven mothers specifically mentioned alcohol as a precipitating factor in their first experience of intercourse:

"I think alcohol had a lot to do with all our downfalls." [1]

" ... if it were left to me, I wouldn't have done ought. But when you're drunk. I only slept with his Dad once and I were pregnant." [2]

Indeed, four of the mothers linked alcohol to their pregnancy. But given the relationship (discussed below) between 'missed pills' and conception, it is probable that heavy drinking was a contributory factor in even more conceptions.

Quite a number of single and cohabiting mothers, nevertheless, reported that their first experience of sexual intercourse had 'just happened'.

"It just happened. I said no twice and then it were the third time." [1]

"It just happened. I didn't especially want to have sex." [2]

Four cohabiting mothers, and just two single mothers, spoke more romantically of sex as the natural consequence of an increasingly close relationship, or as an unplanned but scarcely unexpected development:

" ... I thought the time will be right for me and I'll know when it's right. I think we knew that it was going to happen ... it was more planned than like a surprise to us." [1]

" ... it were just natural anyway 'cos I'd been going out with him a couple of years ... I mean steps came closer and closer and then all of a sudden that were it." [2]

Two single mothers admitted they agreed to sex out of curiosity. One other, however, referred to sex as a means of feeling wanted and loved:

" ... I'd never felt loved as a youngster. I got my love from giving my body to all those men you know, 'cos for one night I felt loved." [1]

Four mothers mentioned specific regrets about the age at which they had begun to have sex:

"I wish I had have waited longer before I'd had sex ... find the right person. Someone to settle down with." [1]

"I wasn't proud of myself but it happened and I couldn't turn back the clock." [2]

Contraception

All the mothers had some knowledge about contraception and all but two of the single lone mothers had actually used it at some time. Never having used contraceptives was more common among the cohabiting mothers – four out of 12. Fewer of the women had used contraception at first intercourse, but even so, almost half of the single lone mothers and just over half the cohabiting mothers had done so.

Those who had never used contraception were:

- One single and one cohabiting mother who had formerly been living in local authority care where they said they were denied access to contraception.[1]

- One single and one cohabiting mother who said they did not mind getting pregnant.

- Two cohabiting mothers who had thought 'it wouldn't happen'.

The influence of alcohol, unplanned sexual intercourse and a feeling that they could 'get away with it' emerged among the factors that had most commonly led to unprotected sexual intercourse:

"My Mum kept telling me to go on it (the pill) … didn't have to, didn't need to … 'cos I wasn't going to do anything." [1]

"He was aggressive and just threatened me into it really, bullied me and I just gave in … I thought 'just this once it will be okay' … and I was irresponsible." [1]

Anxiety about the consequences could, in these circumstances, be more of an afterthought than a forethought:

" … once it had happened then I started to think about it and I started getting worried." [1]

" … after a few times I did start to think, what if I get pregnant and I started getting worried then … Nowt was ever said about it." [2]

" … afterwards … I went to the doctor and asked for the pill." [1]

Risk taking, often thought of as a hallmark of adolescence, was precisely how one cohabiting mother interpreted her behaviour:

"In my head I was thinking, I should not be doing this because I could get pregnant … But … at that age, you want to experiment to see what it is like … and the fact that it's dangerous … makes it more like exciting." [2]

Difficulties obtaining contraception had been a common experience for both the single lone and cohabiting mothers. The barriers included their own embarrassment, anxiety about a lack of confidentiality, parental disapproval, medical reluctance, cost and lack of access:

" … I used to think … the doctor would tell my Mum … they say the doctor is private and that but you always think they're going to tell your Mum or your Dad." [1]

"I asked me mum if I could go ont' pill when I were 15 … she gave me a good hiding … I were just coming up to 16 but she wouldn't let me go on t'pill." [1]

"I wouldn't have been to buy them (condoms) … the embarrassment, just not the thing to do." [1]

" … you could go to the family planning in town … I didn't want all that … talking to a stranger … I felt stupid. I thought they would tell me off. That's why I didn't go." [2]

" … when I was 15 before I got pregnant, I asked to go on the pill … my social worker said no." [2]

Yet two single and two cohabiting mothers reported receiving positive treatment when they sought contraceptive advice from their doctor or family planning clinic:

"I went to my Doctor and asked him. He was great. He advised just an ordinary pill." [1]

"I went with my friend … If I'd have gone on my own I wouldn't have gone for it, but she came with me." [2]

Others were unabashed about buying contraceptives for themselves:

"I had some (condoms bought from Chemist) that doesn't bother me 'owt … I think it's stupid if you don't have any. I've always got 'em in me handbag." [1]

In a number of cases, the mothers' own mothers – and in one case a grandmother – had been instrumental in getting contraception. Three single and three cohabiting mothers said that they had been 'put on the pill' in this way.

The women often admitted they had found it difficult to talk to their boyfriends about contraception, even when they were anxious not to conceive. This tended to be less true of cohabiting than single lone mothers:

"I were worried in case I were pregnant … I didn't want to lose him so that was probably why I didn't say nothing." [1]

"I was too shy to say anything. I don't know what I was shy about. I just was." [2]

Others suggested that contraception was not discussed because their partners did not see it as their responsibility:

" … He said he liked me … but if he did he would have worn one wouldn't he?" [1]

"I was quite, you know, shy really and so if the bloke didn't bring it into the conversation … I never used to say a dicky bird … stupid." [1]

"I think they expect the girls to be on the pill." [1]

Not everyone, however, found discussing contraception a problem:

"Me and D we were so close that we could talk about anything." [1]

"He asked me if I was on the pill" (and suggested he use condom as she was not). [1]

"We had a talk to see ... what was best for us and we both decided I would go on the pill and I was taking the pill. I was scared of getting pregnant." [2]

Conception

Of the 31 young mothers, just seven said their first pregnancies were planned – three who were single lone mothers at the time of interview and four who were cohabiting.² Explanations for the remaining, unplanned conceptions could be divided into four categories:

- failure to use contraception;

- contraceptive failures;

- inadequately used contraception;

- continuing 'myths' about conception.

* Among the *single lone mothers,* 10 of the unplanned conceptions had been a result of incorrect use of contraception or contraceptive 'failures'. Most of these involved the pill. In six cases, however, no contraception had been used.

* A similar number of *cohabiting mothers* had not used any form of contraception at conception. A smaller proportion reported contraceptive failures relating to the pill.

One mother attributed her pregnancy to a split condom, but cases of contraceptive failure relating to the pill were more common. These had mostly resulted from vomiting, diarrhoea or the use of antibiotics that inhibited the pill's effectiveness:

"I went on (the) pill but it made me so sick so I think I was throwing it back up and it weren't working." [1]

" ... I don't think I fully understood the side effects ... if you're on antibiotics – that was my down fall." [1]

" ... I thought take this pill and you won't get pregnant ... you just assume that it's going to work ... I were poorly ... diarrhoea and sickness." [2]

Not taking the pill correctly was a further cause of conceptions:

" It was when I changed from the mini pill to the proper pill I fell with him. I was told to

wait until my next period started ... and I started taking them straight away." [1]

"I forgot to take it for about two days and I'd forgotten all about it and then the next thing I knew I was pregnant." [2]

Teenage 'myths' about sex had also played their part in a few cases. Two young women confessed to thinking they would be safe 'just once':

"I always thought, nothing will ever happen to me ... I'm only young ... I won't get pregnant." [1]

"I thought, once, you won't get pregnant, no diseases or anything ... she (a friend) never fell pregnant and I thought its not going to hurt me." [1]

Comparisons with the childless teenagers

Among the most striking differences between the eight sexually active teenagers interviewed and the young mothers was the former's self confidence and lack of embarrassment about the whole topic of sexual activity and contraception.

They seemed better informed about the consequences of unprotected sexual intercourse and better prepared to take the necessary precautions. All but one had used contraception at first intercourse and three insisted on their boyfriends using condoms even though they were taking the pill themselves:

" ... we knew it were going to happen, so we planned it and got contraceptives ... We'd agreed on it anyway, we'd made sure that we would use one ... I didn't want to get pregnant". [3]

"I was on the pill anyway and we used a condom as well ... So I felt safe ... it protects me both ways." [3] (On the pill for period pains.)

" ... I wouldn't have sex without a condom because there are too many STDs flying around." [3]

On the other hand three teenagers admitted to having had unprotected sexual intercourse at least once:

"Once I didn't have none ... I thought no this isn't right ... I just don't want to risk it." [3]

One of the three clearly shared the same, mistaken beliefs about first intercourse as some of the mothers:

Single lone mothers: problems, prospects and policies

"I didn't know that you could like get pregnant straight away ... I think it was the third time and my cousin said to me to go to the clinic and get a morning after pill ... and when I was there they said, 'oh, do you want to go on the pill?' So I said 'all right then'." [3]

Generally, however, the teenagers were more likely to have discussed contraception with their boyfriends and appeared better able to resist any pressure to have unprotected sex:

"I've said ... I'll have sex with you but you're going to use a condom." [3]

" ... he used a condom ... if he'd refused I would have said no way and I'd have left." [3]

Some had found, in any case, that using a condom was the usual practice of young men or one with which they were happy to comply.

" ... no one's ever asked me, they've just automatically used a condom." [3]

" ... I'd just say to them, have you got something ... I always had so you know that was lucky ... (And they were) happy to go along with ... I don't remember having no hassle at all." [3]

Commentary

As school pupils, many of the mothers had felt that by the time they received sex education at school they 'knew all about it' from their friends, family or other sources. But it is far from clear how much they actually knew and whether it was soundly-based.

It, nevertheless, seems that school sex education for some had come too late – when they were already sexually active. Moreover, the little that the young women did remember about their formal sex education suggested that it was either insufficient or had proved difficult to put into practice. In particular, there had been an obvious gap between a theoretical knowledge of contraceptives and several of these women's ability to use them.

Their experiences suggest that school based sex education needs to be complemented by less formal and more flexible sources of (reliable) information. A few of the young women had been helped by their parents, but this was unusual. They had felt even less well informed about the realities of single lone motherhood and suggested that had they been it might have averted their own.

Most of the mothers had their first experience

of sexual intercourse between 15 and 17 and had conceived within a year. A half of the single lone mothers had felt pressured into first intercourse and alcohol was often a precipitating factor. A number of mothers regretted their early sexual activity.

The pressures of adolescence and developing sexuality, by their very nature, meant that sexual intercourse was not always planned and that, when it happened, contraceptives were not always to hand. Going on the pill in advance of sexual activity was rare. Furthermore, the circumstances under which intercourse sometimes occurred – after drinking – reduced both natural caution and the ability to use contraception effectively. Alcohol consumption may well have explained why so many young women forgot to take their pills or, in some cases, rendered them ineffectual through sickness.

Contraceptive use was complex and did not follow a simple, straightforward pattern. Despite this, only four mothers who did not want to conceive had never used contraceptives and a half of all the mothers had used contraception at first intercourse. There were difficulties gaining access to contraception and a number of mothers had been unable to find a pill that suited them. Different methods, of varying reliability were used at different times.

Nor did contraceptive use necessarily continue once it had begun. In one case a woman had stopped taking the pill following the end of a relationship, but then been 'caught' unprotected when a new relationship started. For young mothers such as these the pill was no guarantee of protection against pregnancy.

While condoms were commonly used, the young women did not always have the necessary self-confidence to insist that their partners use one.

In a few cases, women had been urged by their own mothers, and indeed grandmothers, to seek contraceptive advice. Ironically, those wanting their daughters to 'go on the pill' included former teenage mothers who were anxious that their daughters should not become teenage mothers themselves.

The childless teenage women seemed both better informed about sexual activity and contraception and more self-confident in handling these in their relationships.

Notes

1   They may, of course, have been under 16 years old at the time.

2   See Chapter 7 for more details about the planned pregnancies.

6 Pregnancy

The way that young women respond to discovering they are pregnant will be influenced by many factors, not least their age, maturity, attitudes and personal circumstances. The attitudes of parents, partners and the wider community, may also affect their response. The survey mothers were asked about the influences on their own decisions to continue with the pregnancy and become teenage parents.

Finding out

Their immediate reactions to their pregnancy were, not surprisingly, directly related to whether the conception was planned. Those who had wanted to become pregnant were pleased, even if they were apprehensive:

"I was pleased but scared ... I weren't really young ... I'd had a good time, ... so I looked at it like well I had had a bit of life before I met him."[1]

Shock and anxiety were the common responses among the larger number of teenagers for whom conception came as a surprise:

"... I just thought I'm not that stupid to get pregnant – how can I be pregnant, I've been taking my pill every day ... I was absolutely gutted."[1]

However, the fact that a pregnancy was unplanned did not necessarily mean a baby was unwanted:

"I started getting really worried ... (but) ... I had a lovely pregnancy (and felt) I can't wait 'till I have this baby ... it was going to be good ... good fun ... looking after the baby."[1]

"I were more bothered about what me Mum and Dad'd say ... the responsibility didn't bother me whatsoever. I knew I'd cope and I knew that I'd be all right."[2]

Such feelings were in contrast, in the mothers' accounts, to reactions from some of the fathers. Two were reportedly unprepared to accept any responsibility whatever:

"Not another little brat."[1]

"... 'all right I'll see you later.' That was that ... 'I can't handle that'."[1]

On the other hand, many more were said to be 'happy' when told of the pregnancy. Among these were men who had a continuing, if not yet cohabiting, relationship with the mother:

"... a bit shocked but ... he said that he wanted the baby ... he was fine."[1]

"... he just told me not to worry, everything would be all right ... I'll go home and tell my Mum and Dad."[1]

More surprisingly, an equal number of fathers who no longer had a relationship with the mother were also reported to have been pleased:

"... he was like over the moon and went round telling everyone how he was gonna be a dad."[1]

It did appear, however, that delight at fathering a child did not automatically translate into being happy with the role and responsibilities of fatherhood. As one mother explained;

"... he was over the moon to start with. He really wanted the baby until he realised what kind of life he would have to live."

Telling parents

Some mothers were especially anxious about how their families would react – with justification:

"He (her father) wern't pleased but he never lectured me he just said 'Right, you've made your bed, lie in it, get on with it. She (her mother) went crackers ... swearing at me ... saying I was stupid."[1]

"My nan just broke down in tears. She just couldn't believe it which did made me feel awful ... she's done everything for me ... in a way I felt like I'd let her down ... I didn't actually have a father around and I didn't have a place of my own and it was obvious I

was going to bring this baby up on the dole."[1]

But anger and dismay were not the universal reactions:

"... both sets of parents took it good, really good."[1]

"... I've let them down – they were brilliant though ... they didn't say a bad word to me ... they really helped me through because I was so upset."[1]

Most (three-quarters) of the teenage mothers had mothers who had, themselves, given birth to a first child when they were teenagers.[1] It was, therefore, to be expected that some reactions reflected the extent[2] to which history was repeating itself:

"She were all right because she were the same age when she had me, so she understood what I were going through."[2]

"... she just laughed ... having had them young herself and being in the mess that she was, she wasn't in the position to comment."[1]

Even initial dismay could turn to pleasure as the prospect of becoming a grandparent drew nearer. One grandmother-to-be dramatically returned to speaking terms just two months before the baby was born:

"... after ... she wanted the baby as well and she was looking forward to me actually having the baby because she loved babies."[2]

Deciding against an abortion

Why had the mothers continued with their pregnancies rather than seeking a termination or having their baby adopted?

Both single lone and cohabiting mothers responding to these questions frequently spoke of feeling the need to act 'responsibly' having found they were pregnant. Underlying this was a sense of personal guilt.

"... I don't ever consciously remember making a decision ... I thought I've been damn right irresponsible. I've got to be responsible now."[1]

"... really it were mine and his fault that I were pregnant and so you know it weren't fair

getting rid of a baby when it's not their fault."[2]

Another common factor, as might have been expected, was a rejection of abortion. None of the women claimed to have wanted an abortion and only a small number felt differently with hindsight (Chapter 8).

"... it was like, 'oh no I can't do that' and that was that."[1]

"... I couldn't go through with that, couldn't get rid of a baby, even though its just a tiny little egg before it starts."[1]

"I thought I'm only seventeen I'm going to ruin my life. But I didn't believe in abortions."[2]

"I knew single parents who had had abortions ... they used to say ... 'oh if I had kept it, I wonder what it would be like now'. I thought there is no way I can go through the rest of my life thinking things like that."[1]

Mothers might be accused of taking an anti-abortion stance as a means of justifying their single motherhood. But the way in which the survey women expressed themselves suggested strong and genuinely-held convictions. As one mother whose family had wanted her to have a termination, put it:

"... I couldn't go for that ... I know I couldn't cope with another one but I just know I couldn't get rid of it ... it's not the baby's fault is it ... I just couldn't do it."[1]

Two women were influenced by their own previous experience of a termination:

"... I regretted the first one ... there's no way I'm doing it again ... I made a mistake."[1]

"I'm really against it more so now because I have had one and I would never have it done again."[2]

Only six of the mothers had entertained the possibility of terminating their pregnancy. But even then, it did not seem to have been a 'real' option for four of them:

"I had to go and see a counsellor because I had like two days to decide whether I was going to keep the baby ... I think deep down I knew that I was going to keep it."[1]

"He (the doctor) talked to me (about) the options and I said 'oh I'm keeping it'. I mean I knew straight away."[1]

Just two mothers had seriously considered an abortion :

"I had seriously thought about not having him, but with children I've always been such a soft touch ... I did seriously think about it ... I broke my heart over the decision."[1]

"... I had arranged to have an abortion. I'd been down to (the) doctors and he'd made me an appointment and like, the day before I was supposed to go, I changed my mind."[1]

Although opposed to abortion at the time, other mothers did allow there were circumstances in which they might agree to a termination.

"I'm totally against abortions, always have been ... may be if there was something really seriously bad with the child."[1]

"... if I got pregnant now I would have an abortion 'cause I wouldn't be able to cope with any more children ... at the time I just thought well I can't do it."[1]

Outside influences

For four mothers at least, the decision to keep their babies was reinforced by perceptions of social stigma attached to abortion:

I think if I'd have had an abortion it'd be worse ... people look at you ... I think then you'd have got the dirty looks – oh, you know, she got rid of her baby. Whereas I didn't get any dirty looks when I decided to keep her.[2]

"... one minute I was convinced I was going to have an abortion and people cursing me, slagging me down, next minute I'd ... change me mind again."[1]

"I think you're encouraged to have your baby ... you see the debates on TV ... where the majority are against it. And so people feel afraid to opt for that option."[1]

A few mothers mentioned the influence of religion:

"... I think the only pressure was from him (her boyfriend) – he didn't agree with abortion 'cause he was a Catholic."[1]

"... my dad don't agree with 'em, 'cos we're Catholic ... I think some of it were to do with (that)."[2]

But more general references to anti-abortion attitudes among family members may also have reflected religious beliefs:

"... she told me if I wanted to have an abortion I could but she didn't think that was right either ... I think my mother had a big effect on my decision."[1]

"It was my auntie made me change my mind ... most of my family would have turned against me."[1]

This was by no means typical, however. Many more instances were reported of young mothers deciding to keep their babies against the advice of family and friends:

"... everyone said well have an abortion ... I said 'No, no I can't do that ... but I got involved with the Life people as well and they are all anti abortions aren't they."[1]

"... it was my decision ... my Mum said to me 'you'll have to get rid of it' and I said 'no I won't'."[2]

Two mothers who subsequently cohabited, were especially vehement about their determination to have their babies:

"I was determined I was going to have the baby no matter what anyone said ... I knew in my own head that I wanted to keep it."[2]

"I wasn't going to have an abortion whether he liked it or not ... Sod him, I'm keeping it."[2]

Just a few mothers found their parents were not inclined to put pressure on them one way or another. Such even-handedness was not always appreciated:

" ... think about it, whatever you want to do, it's up to you, but just think about what it's going to do to your life'."[1]

"... me Mum and Dad just asked me what I wanted to do, whether I wanted to keep it ... that's the only time I were ever asked."[2]

"... everyone said it's entirely up to you and I just wanted someone to say either to keep it or get rid of it ... everyone had always told me how to do this, how to do that, and then all of a sudden ... I had to do it all myself."[1]

Free to choose?

None of the women interviewed claimed their choice had been restricted by ignorance of the available options when they became pregnant.

"I had all the choice I wanted ... I wasn't forced into keeping her and I wasn't forced into having an abortion."[1]

"I could have done something about it ... He (the doctor) said if I wanted an abortion he could help me out."[1]

On the other hand, by the time they knew they were pregnant, two-thirds of the mothers had missed one or two periods. This may have left them little time in which to acknowledge the conception and reach their decision on abortion before they felt the pregnancy to be too advanced for a termination to be acceptable. Moreover, if mothers felt that their families and local communities were opposed to abortion, termination might never have been a genuine option. Only one mother, however, questioned whether she had been presented with a real choice:

"I wouldn't have got rid of her but ... the only person that did ask me were the doctor ... I think everyone else just assumes that you are going to keep it ... I'd say there was no choice really."[2]

Help at hand

Most single lone mothers and almost a half of the cohabiting mothers had anticipated help during pregnancy and maternity from their parents:

"My Mum said ... you can stay at home with us ... so I always thought I'd stay with them and I did until she was about six months old."[1]

"... you can stay here as long as you like ... This is your home ... we're not kicking you out."[1]

Only one mother had proved wrong in her assumption:

"I was just totally wrong ... she just threw a frying pan at me."[1] (The mother left home).

For two single lone mothers and three cohabiting mothers this support had played a part in their decision on abortion:

"I'd made an appointment to have an abortion and me Mum and Dad are saying to me 'we'll help you', you know because they wanted me to have him."[1]

"... if she had turned her back on me when I'd gone to tell her I was pregnant then I would definitely have taken steps towards a

termination. *I don't think I'd have been strong enough to go through with it on my own."[1]*

Adoption

Adoption was rarely considered and when it was, mothers found they could not contemplate giving away their babies.

"I could not stand knowing that my baby was with someone else and somebody else caring for it."[1]

Commentary

Most pregnancies were unintended and most mothers were shocked to discover that they were pregnant and anxious about the consequences. The contrast with the pleasure of the few whose pregnancies were planned was unmistakable.

It was also interesting to be told that so many of the children's fathers had been pleased. This initial sense of pleasure did not necessarily translate into committed fatherhood.

While the parents of some mothers were unwaveringly displeased – and more still suggested abortion – many later came to look forward to being grandparents. It is hard to know whether these parents were simply making the best of a *fait accompli* or whether their attitudes represented a sea change from their own youth when extra-marital births were stigmatised and 'shotgun' marriages were the favoured solution.

The attitudes that persuaded the mothers to keep their babies were complex and difficult to disentangle from the influence of others. For whatever reasons, however, they nearly all expressed strong, anti-abortion views. They did not have terminations and most would not choose abortion in the future. Some had resisted pressure from their own families to terminate their pregnancies and one mother had backed out of an abortion after an appointment had been made.

There were other mothers, however, whose families were opposed to abortion. A number also believed that abortion would be more frowned upon in their local communities than giving birth as a single lone mother. By no means all, moreover, had received independent advice on abortion from health professionals.

Even so, there was no sign that the decision to see the pregnancy through was taken lightly and the women had constant worries about how they would cope emotionally and practically as teenage parents.

In the light of the attitudes revealed by the

survey, the question of whether the mothers had enough time to consider having their pregnancy terminated takes on a different meaning. It is not simply a matter of calculating the number of weeks between acknowledging their pregnancy and the time limit on abortion. A more important consideration is the myriad influences that have come into play by the time they had had to 'decide' one way or another. For some teenagers, deeply worried about the attitudes of others, it may already be too late to contemplate so emotionally charged an act as abortion.

Notes

1   About a quarter were married before conception and a half married after conception. Longitudinal research confirms that the daughters of teenage mothers are more likely to give birth in their teens than other young women. (See Kiernan, K.E., 1995).

2   Reflecting the patterns of previous generations, the mothers of the survey women were mostly married by the time they gave birth. One mother who had never married was reported by her daughter as saying '...it's the worst mistake of your life getting married.' [2]

Relationships

Personal relationships are dynamic, not static. 'Snapshot' data, describing how individuals or couples are living at a particular point in time cannot, therefore, tell the whole story. A woman classified by a survey as a 'single lone mother' could, for example, have a well-established relationship with the father of her child and be about to embark on a long and stable cohabitation with him. The label 'cohabitation' might, equally, apply for the moment to a relationship under such severe stress that within weeks it will have broken down.

This chapter examines relationships as a process and considers how the survey mothers had 'got to be where they were' at the time of interview. In so doing, it compares and contrasts the attitudes and relationship patterns of the single lone mothers with those of the cohabiting mothers. Comparisons are also made with the experiences of the sexually active, but childless teenagers who were interviewed.

Single lone mothers

Most of the single lone mothers (14 out of 19) in the survey were no longer in a relationship with the father of their first child. Of the remainder three mothers reported continuing good relations with the father and one couple were trying to re-establish a relationship that had broken down. Unplanned pregnancies had mostly occurred in relationships where no assumptions had been made about their permanence – in other words, 'with a boyfriend'. Thus, while some mothers tried to establish a long-term relationship, others knew from the start that their relationship had no such potential. They took the view that to try and fail at forming a relationship with the father would not necessarily be good for their child:

"... I knew that I would be very unhappy with him and I knew that a child would obviously be very unhappy with him as well ... and so it was never an option.."[1]

One conception, for example, had resulted from a 'one night stand' and another from an unwilling

sexual relationship with a foster father. One woman did not know she was pregnant when the relationship ended.

Conceptions mostly occurred within a few months of the start of a relationship (the range was from a few weeks to more than a year). They had usually known each other for some time before they started to 'go out' together and sexual intercourse did not necessarily take place at the beginning of the relationship.

Relationships that ended

Physical violence brought seven relationships to an end. Assaults had commonly started before conception and, in some cases, continued during pregnancy

"(he) ... threatened to kill me"[1];

"... he was aggressive, he was violent ... he drank ... I was terrified of him, absolutely scared stiff."[1]

"... we thought the baby had died."[1]

One father was forbidden by a court order from seeing his child. In the circumstances, it seemed remarkable that the women had endured such relationships for as long as they did. One young mother justified her continuing relationship as:

"I didn't want her to grow up without having a dad."[1]

Violence featured in all but two of the five cases where the mother had brought the relationship to an end. It was as common, however, for the mothers to report that the impetus had come from the fathers. This was often against the mothers' own hopes and wishes, and was attributed o the men's unwillingness to 'settle down' and face the demands of fatherhood. In some cases, the break up had not occurred until some time after the baby was born:

"... he didn't want to settle down with a baby and that. He wants his freedom too much. I would have gone back with him."[1]

"... he couldn't cope with being a father so he up and went ... I find it really difficult on my own ... because I was expecting his Dad to always be there ... he just felt he had so much responsibility towards us ... all his money."[1]

"I wanted to stop with him. I wanted to get engaged and married like we'd always said."[1]

Walking away from their child was not, as one mother pointed out, an option that the mothers were free to take:

"... I thought, he's never going to grow up ... I've got to look after R (their child). I can't be gallivanting off all over with me mates."[1]

As previously observed, there was a discrepancy between the pleasure which some men displayed on learning they had fathered a child (Chapter 6) and their subsequent behaviour. One mother described the change that took place after their baby was born:

"... he was over the moon ... he didn't really grow up as such until after the baby ... was born. I don't think he realised the responsibilities – it hadn't sunk in how much his life was gonna change."[1]

The minority of single lone mothers whose pregnancies had been planned included one engaged couple who had enjoyed a good relationship even after their baby was born. Subsequently, however, it had deteriorated and become violent. The relationship of another couple did not survive after the father had to move to another area for employment. A third mother had wanted to conceive and been trying to have children for more than a year. She claimed to be little concerned whether her relationship with the baby's father continued, but also reported that he had been violent.

Altogether nine of the 19 lone mothers who were single at the time of interview had cohabited at some stage in their relationships with the fathers. In two out of three cases, it appeared that cohabitation had been the response to pregnancy in the same way that previous generations might have agreed to a 'shot-gun' marriage. Six couples had lived together on their own and three couples had cohabited in the homes of one or other of their families.[1] One woman attributed the subsequent breakdown of their cohabitation to the numerous demands of young parenthood:

"... I think it was the pressure of having your first home, having your first child, having to live together with a partner ... everything mixed together in one dose was just not good, especially when you're so young ... if we'd done things a bit at a time ... if we'd been living together first and then had a baby it might have been better."[1]

Relationships that continued

The single lone mothers who reported a good continuing relationship with the child's father were not – by definition – cohabiting at the time of interview. Their view of those relationships, nevertheless, appeared optimistic, if cautious. All mention the future possibility of cohabitation leading to marriage:

"... it's always like in a few years time when we're a bit older ... and when we've got a bit more money behind us."[1]

"... we plan to ... when J goes to Nursery and I can get a job and then we can get a house together all three of us ... we'll probably live together first ... get married a few years later."[1]

"... if we rush into it we might regret it. But if we wait a couple of years we've got a better chance."[1]

Attitudes to cohabitation and marriage

Although the mothers might have aspired to 'permanent' relationships, they had not necessarily felt ready to commit themselves because they found themselves pregnant. On the contrary, a number plainly considered an unplanned baby was a poor foundation for any long-term commitment:

"We both didn't want to get married at that time because we'd only been going out a few months"[1]

"I never considered staying with him and marrying him just for that."[1]

"... if it had been five or six years on before I'd had the kids then maybe."[1]

"I think I would have thought of marrying him ... but ... I was only young (15) ... It was only a dream really."[1]

When single long mothers spoke of their hopes for a lasting relationship, it was often in terms of a 'trial' period of cohabitation leading, potentially, to marriage.[2]

"... you don't really know that person until you have lived with them ... it's really like a trial run and you should know that person totally before you marry."[1]

"I would settle for just living together ... I would like to get married ... I've always been a romantic ... I've wanted this big lavish wedding dress and Church wedding and big party afterwards ... I suppose I would know that he really is committed to me."[1]

"... it's not imperative that I do get married ... I'd just like to have the day ... the wedding, you know."[1]

But there were others who expressed strong reservations about marriage – often connected to their anxieties about divorce.

"... although I would like to get married ... I've got a very dim view about marriage ... I've seen so many split up ... at an early age that that's one thing I would never rush into."[1]

"... I'm not getting married ... 'Cos I've just seen too many people arguing and splitting up when they get married."[1]

Others regarded marriage, for better or worse, as making it more difficult to bring a failed relationship to an end:

I think I'd rather live with them than get married ... You have to file for divorce ... but if you live with them you can just kick them out."[1]

"You're not committed to them if you're just living with somebody. You can just pack your bags and go. You're not tied down."[1]

Previous experience, including that of a violent boyfriend, had not only made some of the single lone mothers cautious about marriage but relationships in general.

"I don't think I really want another relationship, not yet anyway. I do want one but I just want to find the right person."[1]

"I don't want anybody living with me not for a long time. That's all I can manage, a few nights a week with somebody."[1]

Subsequent relationships

Seven mothers, nevertheless, talked about relationships with men that had followed those with the father of their first child. Four of these had broken down by the time of interview; although

two couples were reportedly trying to repair their rift.

Only one mother mentioned the possibility that already having a child might make it harder to form a subsequent relationship:

"They usually run a mile, men, when they know you've got children."[1]

The fact that more than a third of the single lone mothers had been in subsequent relationships suggested that they had not, in any general sense, 'given up on men'. Like the others who were interviewed, however, they were undoubtedly wary.

Cohabiting mothers

Of the twelve cohabiting mothers, nine were living with the father of their first child and three were in a subsequent relationship. By contrast with the single lone mothers, the majority experience was of positive relationships. They generally defined their relationships as having been good before conception and as continuing in much the same way through pregnancy and early parenthood.

"We were really close we was getting on well ... and we carried on as normal ... nothing changed"[2]

One father was described as having overcome his initial inclination to 'duck' his 'responsibilities' :

"... he didn't want to be rushed into responsibility ... he was just getting used to his freedom ... he said I'll stand by you but don't blame me if I can't cope ... he thought it was the only decent thing to do."[2]

Like the single lone mothers, however, most of the conceptions to mothers in cohabiting relationships were 'accidental'. Just four pregnancies could be described as planned:

"We both just said we'd like to have one 'cos we knew we wanted to stay together then."[2]

"I wouldn't have done it otherwise ... I wanted my child to have a father with him as well."[2]

Living as a couple

Cohabitation for all the couples had followed rather than preceded conception. But while all bar one of the couples were living independently at the time of interview, half had cohabited at some stage in the home of their own or their partner's parents.

As the mothers described it, the wish to cohabit had arisen at the time they discovered they were pregnant or soon after:

"... I said can M (her boyfriend) stay after we had the baby, 'cos he didn't want to be a part-time dad you know. I want us to be together when the baby's born."[2]

Lodging with parents was often cramped, inconvenient and a potential source of tension where partners – and for that matter babies – were concerned:

"... you're living in each other's pockets ... me Mum were interfering ... That were the worst two years I've ever known."[2]

Given the difficulties encountered in obtaining independent housing (see below) it might be a case of 'needs must' to begin with. But access to accommodation was quite clearly one of the factors that had helped these cohabiting relationships to become established.

Breakdown and re-partnering

Three of the mothers were not cohabiting with the father of their first child when interviewed, but with a subsequent partner. Their first relationships, appeared to have broken down in very similar circumstances to those described by the single long mothers:

"... when it did happen you did not see him for dust ... he did not want nowt to do with me. He were off like a bullet ... I have never seen him since."[2]

"... I knew deep down he wouldn't have anything to do with J (the baby) so I felt relieved I wasn't actually fooling myself any more."[2]

It was also self-evident that their experiences of single lone motherhood had not deterred them from forming a second partnership. These second relationships had all been established when the mother's first child was still young:

"He thought J (her child from the previous relationship) was brilliant and we got together and we've been together since."[2]

But that is not to say that none of the relationships were without their teething problems -

"He was a bit wary at first but we managed to get through."[2]

"It was hard at first ... But it's settled down ... and its really working out now."[2]

Attitudes to marriage

Four of the 'cohabiting' mothers were, in fact, married by the time of interview and expressed the view that they had done 'the right thing' for themselves and their children:

"... we'd been together for a while and that's the next stage ... I knew I wanted to get married eventually."[2]

"... it gives you that special bond ... knowing that it is for life and there is no backing out. And it is what we wanted."[2]

But a number of those who were 'living together' also held unambiguously positive views of marriage

"I think marriage is more of a commitment."[2]

"I'd feel more secure I think, if I was married – even though it's only a piece of paper, so they say."[2]

"I'd rather have been married and then had them. I think it's better."[2]

Like single lone mothers they also expressed positive views about weddings, suggesting that the cost of getting married was one reason why they had not, so far, married.[3]

"We keep saying we're gonna run off to Gretna Green and do it ... when we can afford it."[2]

"... we want to get married but it's money that's the main thing ... it'd be nice to have a little do ... it's only the money that's holding us back."[2]

Other reasons mothers gave for not marrying their partner at the time they became pregnant referred to their lack of readiness to make the commitment. Their sense of being 'too young' paralleled the views of some single lone mothers. But it had not deterred them from living with the fathers and, in some cases, later marrying them:

"... I wouldn't get married 'cos I said I was too young ... he asked me and I said no ... I were only seventeen ... we'd have ended up splitting up ... I weren't ready in myself to get married ... But I am now (ready) ... he asked me and I just said, yeah ... I want to now"[2/married]

Single lone mothers: problems, prospects and policies

"... I said I just don't feel ready for that yet ... I thought ... I just wanna get having the baby out of the way first so I know what I'm doing ... and then maybe afterwards ... we'll get married."[2]

"I mean me and K lived together first ... I don't think I would have just jumped in and married him."[2/married]

The teenagers

The teenagers in the survey were all sexually experienced and most had current boyfriends. Some of their attitudes to relationships were, however, distinct. Prominent among their concerns was a strong desire to maintain their independence and not be tied down too soon:

"I wouldn't want to make a commitment like marriage (yet)"[3]

"... if I was to get married I'd make sure I was at least in my late thirties ... You're more likely to stay together."[3]

Marriage, in particular, was viewed as a distinctly long-term prospect, unlikely to be reached without a preceding period of cohabitation:

"... I'd rather know them first properly and then get married"[3]

"... if I was to get married I'd always live with them first (to) know what he's like."[3]

This leaning towards cohabitation as a means of testing commitment was generally reinforced by doubts as to the security of modern marriages:

"I don't think I want to get married ... mostly people I know that's married, they end up breaking up."[3]

"I think getting married would be nice but I think living with is the same thing ... it's not so much hassle if you fall out."[3]

"Most marriages end up in divorce ... all the money to get married and the going through the courts to get divorced ... you might as well just live with someone and if you wanted to you could just go your own way."[3]

Other teenagers, although less cynical, spoke of the importance of marrying 'for the right reasons'. Like a number of the single lone mothers – although speaking in theory rather than practice – one young woman declared that she would not marry her boyfriend if she became pregnant:

"... it wouldn't last ... and if we got a divorce it'd upset the child."[3]

Registering the birth

The difficulties of using birth registration data as a guide to parental relationships and living arrangements have already been considered (chapter 2). An opportunity was taken, however, to discover what considerations lay behind the way that babies born to the survey mothers had been registered.

The single lone mothers

Nine of the single mothers had made joint registrations and seven had registered their children alone. The former included all four mothers who, at the time of interview, were in touch with the fathers and hoping to establish a long-term relationship. The single registrations all occurred in circumstances where the mother felt the relationship had no future or had already broken up with the fathers. In most cases the mother, the father, or both, had been positively opposed to a joint registration:

"No, I wouldn't put it on ... 'Cause I knew we wouldn't last and I didn't want to be finished with him and she had his name instead of mine. He said if I didn't put it on that he'd say it wouldn't be his."[1]

One mother whose relationship had broken down thought children had a right to have their father's name on the certificate. She had, even so, been unwilling to re-establish contact with the father to suggest a joint registration.

The question of surnames was also considered important. Some mothers whose children were jointly registered were nevertheless determined that their babies should use their family name, not that of the father. Willingness to allow children to take their fathers' surnames was seen as conditional on a greater degree of 'commitment' entering the relationship.

"... I said as long as your name is on the birth certificate what does it really matter ... we could always change the name later if we did get married."[1]

"... until we're married or whatever I don't really want him to have the last name."[1]

Others, however, had decided on a joint registration even though their relationship with the father was no longer intact. The view taken was that a two parent registration was the right thing and 'natural' thing to do:

"He said, 'I'm her Dad ... I want to be on the birth certificate'. So he came up 'cos I didn't really want a blank space, you know, father unknown."[1].

"I've put him in his Dad's name ... He wanted him in his name as well. I just thought it were the right thing to do, really, for R ... because he knows who his Dad is."[1]

The cohabiting mothers

All but one of the cohabiting mothers had registered their children jointly. But the reasons given for doing so, and the consequences, were many and various. For example, one woman who was cohabiting with her child's step-father, bitterly regretted the fact that her daughter had been registered with her birth father's surname:

"It's the biggest mistake I ever made ... 'cause he doesn't see her now."[2]

Another mother had taken a more wary view of her relationship with the father, insisting that her own surname be used:

"They're in my name but his names on the certificate ... just in case ... we split up."[2]

However, a mother whose cohabitation with the birth father was progressing well, had come to regret her caution:

"... that was the worst thing we ever did. I listened to me Mum, 'you're only young, what if you split up' ... they've both ended up in my name 'till we get married."[2]

Finding a home

There was little doubt that more of the mothers interviewed would have set up home with their partners at an earlier stage had suitable accommodation been available. Many had, however, found they were not allowed to put their names on the waiting list for a council house or flat until they were 18. A number had also discovered that the likely waiting period, once they made the list, was two or more years. As families with dependent children, some of the mothers and their partners might have been entitled to housing under the homelessness legislation. However none had used this route. Indeed, the possibility of doing so had only arisen for one couple and the prospect of life in a bed and breakfast hotel or

hostel while waiting to be housed was clearly not one that appealed. A number of couples had decided to look for private rented accommodation or sought to raise a mortgage, rather than wait:

"... we put down for a council house as soon as I was 18 ... they said two years ... (but) ... we can put you in a bed and breakfast ... Who wants to be shoved in a bed and breakfast? ... Talk about making you split up ... Now we've got our own house and we live together. I find it more easy than living at me mum's."[2]

"... we did try to get a council house but they said we weren't eligible for one so we had to buy ... we didn't really have a choice, it was either, you know, live with his parents or mine and I didn't want that."[2]

One cohabiting mother described numerous moves before and after her marriage before she and her partner finally gave up waiting for a council house and started buying their own home:

"... I put my name down for a council house when I were eighteen ... then it wern't working too well at my mother's. So after we were married we moved to my nan and grandad's ... when I first put my name on they said waiting list was three months. Anyway we didn't get one and when we got married ... I went on a different list. But whereas I was near the top of that list, I'd gone to the bottom of the priority list."[2]

Living with parents

Many of the single lone mothers and even some of the cohabiting mothers had spent at least some time living either with their own parents or those of their partners. It was an arrangement that some saw as having been distinctly to their advantage:

"I didn't really want to move out, I was still too young ... we didn't do anything until after L was born about living together 'cause my Mum said 'You can stay here as long as you want."[1]

'Living at home' was not, however, an option that had been open to all the mothers, nor was it always satisfactory in the long-run (see Chapter 8). One woman had been thrown out by her parents and another had been told that her boyfriend was not welcome. Nor was it the case that all the mothers had been living at home when they became pregnant. One single lone mother had left home to avoid a violent father and another had been thrown out by her parents when she was 16:

"I had a father who was an alcoholic, used to beat me mother up; used to beat us up. So just before my 16th birthday I packed up and left and I've never been back since."[1]

"I was devastated. I was all on my own for the first time in years ... suddenly I'm on my own with the little baby."[1/Mother thrown out of home at 16 when she left school. Went to live in a hostel].

Another single lone mother had taken a decision before she gave birth that continuing to live in the family home was out of the question:

"... there's no way I'd have attempted to bring up children in my mum's house ... it would have meant sharing a room with my little sister ... and I wouldn't want a child of mine in a house where I caught nothing but good hidings ... there's no way she would have put up with a baby."[1]

Commentary

As might have been expected, the relationships of the mothers were not static. Although some were living with the birth fathers of their children, some were single lone mothers, having broken up with the fathers, others were single, but still hoping to form a stable relationship with the fathers. The study included single lone mothers who were in steady subsequent relationships, but as yet not cohabiting, and women who were cohabiting with their children and a stepfather figure.

Indeed, while most single lone mothers were no longer in a relationship with the father of their first child, a half had, at some stage, cohabited with him. Moreover, more than a third had, at some stage, had subsequent relationships. It should, however, be noted that none of the single lone mothers who had a good, *continuing* relationship with their child's father had ever cohabited with them. But they did hope to do so in the future.

All the mothers – whether now single or cohabiting – reported violence in the relationship or the fathers' unwillingness to settle down as the major causes of the breakdown in their relationships. Their experiences had made some of the single lone mothers wary about marriage although this neither precluded it entirely or prevented the establishment of second relationships. By comparison, cohabiting mothers seemed less anxious and more positive about

marriage. Their attitudes may well reflect both their age and their more positive relationship experiences.

Not surprisingly, marriage for the teenage women was a long-term prospect. Moreover, they thought cohabitation was a likely option pre-maritally because of their doubts about the security of modern marriages.

Joint birth registration had been the norm for the children of the cohabiting mothers and for nine of the children of single lone mothers. Mothers often viewed having the father's name on the birth certificate as the 'right' or 'natural' thing to do. Despite this, the children of single lone mothers often bore their mothers' surnames – with a view expressed by some mothers that they would not consider substituting the fathers' surnames in the absence of a committed relationship.

Whether they were a priority for local authority accommodation or not, many mothers had found they could not join the waiting list for a council flat or house until they were 18. Even then, they faced potentially long waits to be housed.

The result was a range of unsatisfactory housing experiences, including cohabiting in the homes of parents or their partners' parents. While 'living at home' was undoubtedly to the advantage of some mothers, the benefit was sometimes short lived. Nor was it an option for women whose parents had shown hostility either to them or to their partners.

Notes

1 Two mothers had cohabited before the conception but the relationship of one had broken down before the baby's birth. For six couples the cohabitation started after conception but before the baby's birth. Two of these relationships ended before, and four after, the baby was born. One couple had cohabited after the birth.

2 See McRae, S. (1993) on the attitudes of cohabiting parents to marriage.

3 Again see McRae, S. (1993).

8 Motherhood

This chapter explores the mothers' experience of parenthood and the amount of support they received. It also reports the women's views of teenage motherhood and the advice that they would offer, with hindsight, to today's teenagers. Relationships between their children and their current partner – whether fathers or stepfathers are also considered.

Experience of motherhood

Most of the single lone mothers said they had found parenthood difficult. There were, however, nuances to their experiences. Most notably, many also talked about their positive enjoyment of bringing up children, so that for most of them motherhood was neither 'all good' or 'all bad':

"I think you get a lot of joy out of having a child but ... they are hard work."[1]

"... it's hard 'cause you haven't got anyone – although I've got close family ... you've got to take on the role of father as well."[1]

For some, high expectations of motherhood had mostly been fulfilled:

"I loved being pregnant. I thought it was brilliant ... had this feeling of being worthy of something and I just felt ... radiant all the time. And I was looking forward to having the baby ... I couldn't wait for this little thing to look after and love."[1]

But not so for others:

"I didn't realise it would feel like it did ... I was so tired ... I wasn't prepared ... I don't think anybody is."[1]

"... it always seemed easy when it was somebody else's and you could give it back ... I just thought it'd be the same."[1]

About a quarter of the single lone mothers specifically mentioned the way in which motherhood had propelled them, unexpectedly, from teenage independence to responsible parenthood – obliging them, as they saw it, to grow up overnight.

"It's sad to change from being a normal teenager to a mum. I feel like I'm missing out – but I wouldn't change it."[1]

"... I've grown up a lot quicker, I've learned to take responsibilities for my actions and responsibility for someone else."[1]

Cohabiting mothers rarely mentioned their loss of teenage independence in the same way and appeared less conscious of the restrictions that motherhood placed on their social lives. It should, however, be remembered that they were generally older than the single lone mothers at the time of interview. Cohabiting mothers were also less likely to mention parenting difficulties:

"... I find it all right ... I don't find it too hard ... I've always had S as well, me partner ... to help me so that were a big help."[2]

"I had no money, I had nowhere to live and I just couldn't face ... up to looking after a baby on my own. But once he came back I was quite happy."[2]

Researchers suggest that young mothers are often not 'prepared' for what is entailed in the care of a baby;[1] nor can they necessarily anticipate its quite different needs as it develops into a child. Some of the survey mothers said they found life with a toddler more difficult and others less so. None, however, appeared to have been taken entirely by surprise:

"I think now is worse than when he were a baby ... he's getting into everything, you've got to be watching him all the time ... so I think it's a lot harder now ... as he's getting older."[1]

"It's better now than when she was a baby."[1]

Money

The project had not planned to explore how mothers managed financially. It was, however, an issue which at least half the mothers raised under the heading of motherhood experiences. Income

Support was the major source of income and the most common observations were about the difficulty of managing on the payments available:

"... money's always a worry but you just cut your cloth accordingly."[1]

"... it's hard to live on ... the money that I get ... being under 18 I get like £20 less than people who are over 18 ... it's not a lot ... you can't have luxuries ... you know."[1]

One mother spoke of the difficulty of adjusting to Income Support, having previously lived on earnings from employment:

"... I thought how am I going to manage and I ain't got no money and people had told me how much they got off social and I thought I wouldn't be able to cope ... from £100 (earnings) to £50 odd – it's a long drop 'cause you've got to keep your baby as well, so it were a bit hard ... You don't get enough to live on, not to pay your bills."[1]

Another woman, who had no work experience took a different view:

"I don't think it's that bad because I've never had money so if someone gave me a hundred pounds I wouldn't know what to do with it."[1]

While paid work might seem an obvious answer to these financial problems, it was not an easy option. Even the few who were working part-time had found that alternative childcare and other necessary arrangements were difficult to make:

"... it's very hard to even try and consider getting a little job ... It's hard to be able to afford to maybe take them on little trips."[1]

"It's hard, but I'm slowly sorting myself out with part-time work."

Money worries were mentioned by only two of the cohabiting mothers. This was likely to reflect the fact that their cohabiting partner was likely to be in employment.

Support from parents

The mothers' own mothers were credited with providing the most (and sometimes considerable) support and practical assistance. This was true whether the women were living at home or independently. More than half the single lone mothers and even more of the cohabiting mothers (at least 10 out of 12) had received such help.

"... she did ask me to move back home again ... living at home with my mum made things a lot easier ... didn't make me pay much rent ... I knew that at night time ... my mum would be there to help me."[1]

"I can go out when I want. My mum's always there to babysit ... She'd always look after S through the night while I catched up on my sleep."[2]

"They'd babysit 40 times a week if I asked. They'd babysit any night."[2]

"Without the help of my mum I don't think I would have coped ... I lived at home until J was 18 months old."[2]

The single lone mothers, especially, mentioned help with babysitting and other childcare; some also referred to financial help:

"... she used to lend me money if I were a bit down on money."[1]

"... they were helping us out financially and getting baby clothes, food and everything – they were just brilliant."[1]

A rather larger minority of cohabiting mothers also mentioned receiving financial assistance from parents:

"P's mum helps ... She like gives us money to go out sometimes ... she'll buy bits of food or she'll give us a couple of quid to put in the telly."[2]

"... As soon as I said I wanted it they started helping me. My dad said ... if you need any money or if you need any help just come to me. And I'll help you out ... it's good to have someone like that."[2]

Among those mothers who had moved out, the loss of readily available help from parents was a frequently mentioned regret:

"I like me own home, I've got me own privacy ... but I do miss living at me mum's ... She used to have him sometimes overnight ... they still have him a lot now."[1]

On the other hand, the dividing line between support and interference could be a fine one, as two mothers testify:

"... she used to say do it like this, dress her like that and after a while it got on my nerves and I had to move out."[1]

"... they were very interfering, she'd sort of bite her tongue now and then ... and I used to

keep saying 'Oh, I just can't wait to get out of here' ... I missed my mum when we first moved in here."[2]

Receiving willing help from parents was not, however, everyone's experience:

"... when I ask them, but I have to ask."[1]

"... she was there for the praised bits, but she wasn't there for the sleepless nights, the teething, not being able to get out."[1]

"... as far as they're concerned ... I've made my bed so I've got to lie in it ... It just seemed that I was on my own totally."[1]

"I was on me own ... I was brought up in care so I didn't have any support from me parents."[2]

Other help

Other sources of help mentioned by the single lone mothers included a local family centre, a foster mother and other mothers living in the same hostel:

"I was quite lucky ... even though I didn't have support from my family ... I were in a hostel for young mothers when I first had J ... we all rallied round together ... they helped me a lot ... told me about their experiences about bringing up a baby."[1]

Four mothers also referred specifically to help from their boyfriends' mothers – while two cited support received from the boyfriends themselves. Grandparents and friends were also mentioned, sometimes as part of the assistance received from an extended family consortium:

"... his sister ... used to come over and talk to me. She used to stay in the house with me till him or his mum came back from work so it weren't so bad ... she either watches him or me mum watches him or S watches him when I go out."[1]

"... I had all my friends and they helped me ... My mum, my auntie and then my cousins would come and take him out and things like that."[2]

"I was living with a full family so there was a lot of help there. So it'd probably be a totally different story if I was on my own."[2]

Sometimes, however, support from extended family and friends had not lasted beyond an initial burst of enthusiasm following the birth:

"... for the first six months of having her it was fine ... people were very willing to babysit for a new baby; but then when it got to the teething stage, the friends disappeared."[1]

"... when I had her I had a lot of help but now she's one ... they don't want to know. And it seems harder for me all the time."[2]

There was less comment than might have been expected about how much or how little help the cohabiting mothers received from their partners. This may be because they were thinking back to early motherhood when most of them were still living with parents. Alternatively, they may have understood the question in terms of the support that they and their partner had received. Those who did describe help from their partner made it clear that it was valued:

"... When I look at my friends ... there's a few what have not got partners with 'em now, and I just don't know how they do it."[2]

"He helps a lot."[2]

"I only had to do it on my own for three months ... because then I met L and L took us on."[2]

Fathers' relationships with their children

Relationships between children and their fathers are often disrupted when the relationship between their parents breaks down. All contact may be lost within a matter of a year or two.[2] It was, therefore, not surprising that about a third of the single lone mothers' children had minimal or non-existent contact with their fathers. Some fathers, for example, had seen their child just a couple of times as a baby.

Good continuing relations were – as might be expected – reported by single mothers who had continuing relationships with the fathers, themselves:

"He comes down every day and see him so it's not so bad."[1]

Regular father-child contact was also reported by the mother who had hopes of repairing her broken relationship:

"... he dotes on him ... something chronic ... they're fantastic together."[1]

But there were other instances where the parents, although living apart, had managed to maintain a relationship that enabled contact to take place:

Single lone mothers: problems, prospects and policies

"... my children do see their Dad every Saturday."[1]

"He is good with R. He does love him. He takes him and that a lot. He comes and sees him a lot."[1]

The same was true of situations where the single lone mother was in a subsequent relationship. Much depended on the ability of the mother and the child's father to tolerate each other:

"I still see her Dad a lot. He has her some weekends and that ... as she gets older he has her like weekends Saturdays he has her and his mum has her like every weekend. She has her all weekend."[1]

But where relations between the estranged parents were marked by acrimony, or dialogue had broken down altogether, children were unlikely to be seeing much of their fathers:

"When it suits him he'll come round for half an hour once every couple of months."[1]

"... he doesn't want anything to do with us ... he tells people that its not my baby."[1]

Despite a long period of absence, one mother insisted she would still allow the father access, for the sake of her child:

"I always wanted him to come and see her ... he never turned up ... he hasn't bothered in the last two years ... Her dad could knock on the door today and I'd still let him in because he's got as many rights to her as I've got."[1]

Stepfathers

Mothers in second relationships were, meanwhile, enthusiastic about the way that their partners were relating to their children:

"Brilliant. Treats him as his own. He's always been good with him – even when we were just friends."[1]

"... probably a better Dad than P could ever have been ... To see them together you wouldn't know it wasn't his little boy."[1]

Mothers who were successfully cohabiting with the father of their child at the time of interview gave, as might be expected, positive accounts of their partners' relationships with their children:

"He felt right proud of being a Dad ... He takes him out ... Feeds him and changes him."[2]

"... he's a part-time worker and every penny goes like on H."[2]

"He was quite overjoyed; he was always there."[2]

Where cohabiting mothers were in a subsequent relationship, however, there were varying accounts of their children's contact with their birth fathers. One mother, who had broken up with her child's father before he even knew she was pregnant reported that:

"He has never seen J – only once and he was twelve months old at the time and he was just going to walk straight past him in the street ... and he has never seen him since."[2]

Another, despite a promising start, said the father had not been in contact since their child's first birthday:

"He was really good with her, especially when we took her home; she cried all night, and he'd sit up with her all night."[2]

As with the single lone mothers, positive feelings about the relationship between their current partner and the children from their first relationships were marked:

"... the first time he came ... him and R started to build a relationship ... He was one of the first people she ever spoke to, 'cause she wouldn't speak to anybody else."[2]

"... he would want to help ... I could not get it into my head that he were trying to ... it were like he were the father."[2]

Hindsight

Looking back, the young mothers were almost unanimous that the teenage years were not the best age to embark on parenthood. One single lone mother said she had positively wanted a baby before she was 20, but the remainder viewed 'twentysomething' as the optimum age:

"... if I'd had a choice ... I would like to have been about twenty-four."[1]

"... I wish we'd been a couple of years older – twenty, twenty-three, twenty-five ... I think I'd have coped better ... I'd have been a lot more grown up."[2]

Nevertheless, a number of mothers – cohabiting more often than single lone – were ready to identify certain advantages to young motherhood.

"If I had to go back I'd have them young."[2]

"When he's eighteen, I'll only be thirty-six ... I can do it all like when he's older."[2]

"I'm going to be young, she's going to be young ... and we're going to have quite a close relationship I think because we're young together."[1]

One mother, however, described herself as an exception that proved the rule:

"I'm glad I had them at a young age but just because it's worked for me doesn't mean it would work for them."[2]

For three single lone mothers, the sense of having started parenthood too early was so strong that they now believed they would have done better to consider an abortion:

"... if I'd listened to my mum and all my neighbours who'd had kids who said you don't want them ... I think I would definitely have had an abortion."[1]

"I think I'd have had second thoughts if I'd have known just how hard it was gonna be."[1]

"I would have had a termination. I know it sounds horrible saying that (because) I wouldn't be stuck here."[1]

Hindsight also exposed one notable difference between the views of single lone and cohabiting mothers – attributable, it seemed, to the latter's more settled relationships. With just two exceptions, the cohabiting mothers insisted that – in spite of knowing what they now knew – they would not have done things differently:

"I got everything I wanted so I don't want anything else."[2]

"I wouldn't change anything now for the world – I wouldn't turn the clock back. I love my children more than anything in the world."[2]

The single lone mothers were more ambivalent about their situation. Almost without exception, however, they were firm in their belief that having had their children, they would not wish to be without them.

Advice for today's teenagers

Almost all the single lone mothers had advice to offer today's teenagers. Most of this related to three specific subjects – sexual activity, contraception and having a baby.

Thus, while some suggested that young women should postpone or limit their sexual activities -

"... put it off."[1]

"Just don't do it."[1]

- there was also a strong view that teenagers should ensure they had good contraceptive protection:

"Be careful ... if I knew then what I know now I'd be straight out and getting on the pill."[1]"

"Make sure the pill works."[1]

"... make sure you're totally prepared, that you've got contraceptives and don't rely on your partner."[1]

None of the women advocated becoming a single lone mother:

"I would strongly advise against someone having a baby so young and not in a stable relationship."[1]

"Don't have that baby and then think what do I do now and where do I go from here – because that's the mistake I made."[1]

Cohabiting mothers, despite their differing circumstances, offered similar advice:

"... I think it should be trendy to be a virgin nowadays. I wish I'd waited – I really, really regretted it – not then but since then."[2]

"I'd advise them to take precautions and be very careful."[2]

"I'll tell her how hard it is to have a baby young – so she doesn't make the same mistakes as I did."[2]

"I'd make sure it didn't happen to her ... You get as far as this ideal picture of you, your boyfriend and the baby ... You don't see the rest of it ... the tantrums, the not having enough money to go and buy a packet of nappies, stuck in night after night."[2]

Single lone mothers: problems, prospects and policies

Commentary

Motherhood, for many of the mothers, was a mixture of hard work and enormous joy. Viewed in those exceedingly general terms, it was unlikely to have differed greatly from the experience of other mothers with their first babies.

Aspects of single lone motherhood were, however, underlined in the survey that set it apart from the experience of cohabiting mothers. Prominent among these were not only the difficulties of caring for a child alone, but also the problem of surviving on a limited income, usually Income Support. The difficulty – impossibility, in some cases – of managing on such limited resources was a central concern.

Some single lone mothers, even so, had received considerable help from their families, boyfriends and friends. Their own parents had in many, but not all, cases provided valuable support. It seems possible that some of these young mothers living at home actually received more help than many first time mothers living independently. But such help did not always continue beyond the initial burst of enthusiasm. The fine dividing line between support and interference sometimes meant that 'living at home' could only be a short-term solution.

That there was often little relationship between children and their birth fathers was not, perhaps, surprising. Less so, given the extent to which the single lone mothers described the fathers of their children as violent and/or reluctant to settle down. What was less expected was the uniformly positive accounts which mothers in subsequent relationships gave of relations between their children and their new partner or boyfriend.

A substantial minority of single lone mothers had experienced unplanned motherhood as an unwelcome jolt into adult responsibilities. Only a few saw any redeeming virtues in being young parents. However, asking the women to look back on their early experiences of motherhood produced mixed and complex reactions. Almost all had accepted their role and would not dream of being without their children. Yet, given the choice, they would often have done things differently. Certainly they would not have chosen to have children at such a young age – and typically not before reaching their mid-20s. The mothers were unanimous in urging today's teenagers not to become young single lone mothers, to use contraception with care and, possibly, even to postpone their sexual activity.

Notes

1   For example, Hudson, F and Ineichen, B. (1991).

2   Bradshaw, J. and Millar, J. (1991).

9 Work and family

Single lone mothers are sometimes depicted as young women whose prospects in terms of education and employment are so poor that they have little to lose by becoming parents at an early age. This chapter explores work and family issues from the mothers' point of view. The experiences of the single lone and cohabiting mothers are considered together.

Education, training and work

At the time they became pregnant, most of the mothers were either in education, on a Youth Training Scheme placement, at work, or were intending to do so. The response, when they told teachers and employers about their approaching maternity had varied. Some schools were found to be helpful in ensuring that they did not lose the chance to gain qualifications.

"... fabulous, even the examiners ... All the tutors, all the girls ... were really good about it."[1]

"... they said I could stay and finish my exams as long as I try to keep in my uniform as much as I could."[2]

A number of women, however, mentioned the mockery of classmates – feared or actual – as a reason for leaving school:

"I went to school for ages ... It was (difficult) when everybody got to find out. I always got to come home in tears 'cos everybody had been getting at me ... It was my head of year that got me into the girls unit."[1]

"I could have gone back to school while I was pregnant but I know that people laughed at me ... But I had a teacher coming round for a month while I was pregnant."[2]

One mother had given up the offer of a university place on finding she was pregnant. Another, less qualified to begin with, had been refused a YTS placement because of her pregnancy:

"(They said) ' ... oh well nobody'll employ you when you're pregnant ... what's the point of training you ... and then you've got to go at the end of it' ... they were no help."[2]

Among those who had already left school when they became pregnant, some had a toe hold – but not much more – in the labour market. Low paid jobs predominated:

"I wanted to be a hairdresser. I'd finished my training course and they didn't keep me on so I didn't have enough experience to get any other work so I just went to work in a factory."[2]

"I also worked as a nursery school helper."[2]

Others, with rather better job prospects had reluctantly felt obliged to abandon them:

"I was hoping actually to stay in ... I missed out by something like four months ... It wasn't possible for me to stay in ... I had no choice but to leave."[1]

"I enjoyed it so much ... the doctor had to sign me off in the end because he knew I wouldn't willingly leave."[1]

"I went for a test and I passed ... and then I found out I was pregnant and I couldn't do it, so it's a bit of a let down."[1]

Parenthood and work

At the time of interview, all but two of the mothers were looking after their children full-time and only one (single lone) mother was working full-time. The majority made it plain that they preferred not to work before their children started school. This reflected both a reluctance to miss out on early development and, in some cases, an unwillingness to leave their children with anyone else while they were so young.

"I would like to get a job but not until ... D goes to playschool, 'cause I'm so frightened of missing out on the first things that they do."[1]

Single lone mothers: problems, prospects and policies

"I could not leave my baby and go out to work."[2]

A number of mothers said they had been offered the opportunity to return to work, but had felt torn between doing so and staying full-time with their babies:

"... I had prospects at the firm ... and I thought I was letting them down as well as myself ... I didn't really want to leave the child for a while and I had to be back by the time the child was three months old."[1]

Others had turned down job opportunities arising since the birth:

"... when I actually had him I decided I couldn't leave him ... I thought, 'oh, part-time mother' it wasn't for me that – I didn't like that idea."[1]

Many, however, intended to resume their education, training or working life once their children were in full-time education.

"I wanted to be a social worker, I still do ... I thought put it on hold for a few years and then go back to it. I shall just carry on where I left off."[1]

"... she's going to be off to school and I can start ... my career then ... I'll only be 20."[1]

"I hope that I'm going to go to College and get myself a job once R's started school. Do something with my life."[1]

"If I don't get a part-time job I'm thinking of going to College for typing. And then I'll definitely have a job."[2]

A number of mothers also acknowledged, with regret, that their early motherhood made such ambitions harder to achieve:

"I've seen people from work – now they've passed this and they've passed that and I think well I've got nothing like that to show for it. And they say you're still young and you could do it anyway, but I don't know."[1]

"... you need GCSEs and stuff like that to get a job ... I didn't have any of that so I can't get a job now."[2]

Single lone mothers were especially likely to cite lost educational or career opportunities as a consequence of their teenage motherhood. But some of the cohabiting mothers expressed similar feelings.

"... I wish I'd had them ten years later. Gone into the RAF like I'd wanted to."[1]

"I would like to have been about twenty-four ... I would have got me certificates and been in a really good job."[1]

Childcare arrangements

One mother had returned to work but subsequently run into childcare difficulties:

"... the grannies were a bit fed up with having them so I had to pack it in."[2]

But she was not the only mother whose (part-time) employment ambitions were being thwarted by the problem of finding reliable childcare that they could afford:

"I'd love to have gone back to work. I would still like to go back to work now if I could find a way of paying for somebody I could trust ... I'd go back to work tomorrow."[1]

"I would like to work ... a couple of hours a day ... (but) ... it wouldn't be worth my while."[2]

The single lone mother who was working full-time was training as a solicitor. To do this she relied on considerable family support:

"My dad and stepmother ... they have him two days a week and he stays, that helps tremendously. It helps financially because I'm not having to pay for childcare those few days ... And I've got an aunty has him one day a week."[1]

Career prospects

The trainee solicitor was one of only a handful of women whose career prospects appeared at all promising. Their common feature was either having qualifications and skills or significant previous work experience.

"I'd like to go back into printing. I was assistant manageress ... I thoroughly enjoyed it."[1]

"... when M goes back to school in September ... I'll be able to go back and it is good money. Making clothes for Marks and Spencer."[1]

Family life

Mothers were asked to compare their actual experiences with the hopes and expectations they had harboured for family life before they became pregnant. To this, almost a third replied that they had not even thought about having children. Given the number of unplanned pregnancies, as well as the mothers' ages, this was not altogether surprising:

"Everyone ... who knew me always thought I would be the last person ever to have children."[1]

"... nothing like that crossed me mind. I just wanted a job and have me freedom."[2]

"I don't think anybody thought about having babies when they were sixteen and seventeen."[2]

But there were at least as many who said they had assumed that they would have children, although not necessarily in the circumstances that they now found themselves:

"That's all I ever wanted when I was young anyway ... two kids, a home and a husband, that'll do me and it has so I'm fine."[2]

More than a third of the single lone mothers specifically mentioned having hoped for a permanent relationship, a settled home and some financial stability before they embarked on parenthood. Some described this as the 'traditional', 'right' or 'proper' way to do things.

"I thought I'd have a nice job ... and get some money first and then get married and have a baby, that way. But it didn't work out."[1]

"I just thought the first thing I'd do is ... work ... then be married first and then have a house and the children – I didn't think it would go the other way round."[2]

"I wish I'd done it like all the right proper way, you know. The old fashioned way of getting married, then children."[1]

Cohabiting mothers were generally less likely to highlight the disparity between past hopes and current circumstances – no doubt, reflecting their more settled situation.

Future hopes

Asked where they would like to be in five years time, almost half the single lone mothers referred to hopes of 'finding a father' for their children, a settled relationship and, preferably, marriage:

"I want to meet somebody so like she's got a father figure around even though she's got her dad ... that's like only weekends. It's not as if he's here constantly."[1]

"I think he needs stability ... he needs some sort of male role model and he's got plenty of granddads – but maybe needs a dad ... he's started asking about dad. He notices he hasn't got a daddy. He asked me why."[1]

"I hope to meet a nice husband, a father to my children."[1]

Cohabiting mothers, for obvious reasons, raised a rather different set of priorities – although weddings (for those who were not already married) were still mentioned:

"I'll probably be married by then ... settling down and planning for another child ... Or I could like get married and find a job."[2]

"... I'd like to be working full-time, have a car, a house and be able to go on holiday. Be a perfect family, I suppose."[2]

The teenagers

The small comparison group of childless teenagers were also asked about their plans and ambitions. While both marriage and children were, in most cases on the agenda, a long lead time was usually assumed.

"... some day when I'm married and like older, sort of nearer thirty ... I've got other things to do, I ... don't want all that responsibility ... it's too big when you're 16."[3]

"My first thought was that I'm not going to get pregnant until I'm at least 25 and I don't know if I ever want to get married."[3]

"I wouldn't mind having children but not 'till I've like really got my career going ... it's going to be like miles away in the future ... probably in my late twenties ... thirties."[3]

"... you can't really do much with your life, can you, when ... you've got a little baby to support? So much responsibility involved ... you wouldn't have a chance to do anything else."[3]

There was, however, one teenager who felt she was already under pressure to get pregnant. So far, she had successfully resisted:

"... all my friends nearly ... have already got kids ... I want a kid, but I haven't got no money ... and I haven't got like a proper stable relationship ... Babies are my weak spot, I just love them ... I'm just using my head ... I don't want to be bringing up a kid and I haven't got nothing to offer it ... I'm trying to look at it from an older person's, from my mum's point of view."[3]

Commentary

What the mothers had to say about their experience of education, training and employment before motherhood did not suggest that they had been leading empty lives – hanging around on street corners, as it were, with nothing better to do than have a baby. On the other hand, there seemed little likelihood, in all but a few cases, that exceptional educational qualifications or career opportunities were likely to come their way. Their prospects in terms of income and opportunities were generally limited. The exceptions were women whose qualifications and skills or work experience would clearly make it easier for them to pursue a career in spite of young motherhood.

In the remaining cases it was all too evident that early parenthood had acted as a barrier to developing their 'human capital' and taking advantage of such opportunities as had existed before they became pregnant. Their occupational prospects and their chances of finding suitable paid work once their children started school were less good than they might otherwise have been.

That being so, it was all the more interesting that so many single lone mothers expressed a strong preference for remaining at home and caring for their children themselves while they were of pre-school age. That they were, as a result, almost invariably financially dependent on social security, did not mean that they were complacent about this dependency. Indeed, all assumed that they would work once their children were in school and a number would prefer to be working part-time now. Practical and financial obstacles prevented them from doing so.

Asked where they would like to be in five years time, half of the single lone mothers volunteered the hope that they would have formed a stable relationship with a man who would be a father to their children. Many had hopes of marriage. Likewise, when asked to compare their current experience with their aspirations before becoming pregnant, at least a third said they had assumed they would have done things the 'proper' way – by which they meant forming a stable relationship, setting up home and establishing an income before starting a family.

10 Conclusions

One of the reasons that single lone motherhood has increased during the past 20 years is that conceptions to young unmarried couples are less and less likely to precipitate marriage. Yet it would be wrong to suppose that the decline of the 'shotgun' wedding means that today's young mothers no longer aspire to stable relationships and two-parent homes for their children. Possibly a few women, old enough to be financially independent, are making positive choices to have babies on their own. But that in no sense describes the young women who were interviewed for this study.

No matter how personally happy they were with their children, the young women took no great pride or pleasure in being lone parents. They had not planned to be young single mothers or, in most cases, to become pregnant so young.[1] And they would certainly not advise today's teenagers to follow their example. They, themselves, would have preferred their family formation to have followed a 'traditional' pattern – setting up home in an established relationship and not having their first child until their mid-twenties. The gulf that had opened up between these aspirations and their experience of relationships that had, for the most part, ended because of the father's violent behaviour or unwillingness to 'settle down' was all too apparent. Even so, their long-term hopes often remained focused on finding a man they could share their lives with, who would be a father to their child(ren). Some mentioned dreams of marriage.

Furthermore, although they were not living with a partner when interviewed, a half of the single lone mothers had cohabited with the fathers of their children *at some time*. These relationships had either broken down between the conception and birth of their baby or in the months and years following the birth. As such, they provided powerful anecdotal evidence in support of the demographic thesis that Mark Brown argues in chapter 2 of this report: that growth in the numbers of single lone mothers is, to a significant degree, an old phenomenon in a new guise. As an increasing proportion of young parents cohabit instead of marrying, so an increasing proportion of single lone mothers will be those whose cohabiting relationships have broken down. Twenty years ago such women might well have married only to have their relationship end in separation or divorce (see chapter 2). Nowadays, however, they find their way into the official statistics as single (never-married) lone mothers instead of lone mothers who are separated or divorced.

Put another way, a growing proportion of single, never-married lone parents can be viewed as the modern equivalents of teenagers in earlier generations whose 'shotgun' marriages ended in failure. It would, therefore, be a serious mistake to suppose that relationship breakdown is a declining cause of lone parenthood. Policy makers, in particular, should beware treating the rise in single lone motherhood as if it were an entirely separate issue of young women having babies on their own. This is far from the case.

Demographic evidence

The scope for misplaced assumptions when interpreting statistics is further demonstrated in the case of birth registration data. This divides births into those (two out of three) registered by married couples, those registered by unmarried couples giving the same address, couples giving a different address and those registered by the mother alone. Not all unmarried mothers have never been married and some births registered by the mother alone may be to unmarried couples who are cohabiting or are about to begin doing so.

Half of today's births outside marriage are jointly registered by their parents at the same address and – as Mark Brown argues – the proportion may not be much lower for never-married mothers and their partners.[2] Indeed, all the cohabiting mothers from the qualitative survey had jointly registered their children as had a half of the single lone mothers. They viewed joint registration as the 'right' or 'normal' thing to do although the children may use their mother's family name in the absence of a committed relationship with the father.

Social and economic characteristics

Some account also needs to be taken of the degree to which the social and economic circumstances of single lone mothers who have and have not cohabited previously may differ. The General Household Survey data analysed in Chapter 3 did not allow this to be directly established. But some important findings emerged. Cohabiting couples are not as well off on a range of social and economic characteristics as married couples. But cohabiting, two parent families are generally better off than single lone mothers. Ex-cohabiting single lone mothers may either constitute a 'better off' group within the ranks of single lone motherhood or their circumstances may worsen when their cohabitations break down.

The qualitative research

The 31 mothers in the qualitative research for this report were chosen because they had all been single, never-married teenagers when their babies were conceived. As such, they had all been 'at risk' of single lone motherhood. But by the time they were interviewed, almost two-thirds had cohabited with the father at some time, including almost a half of the 19 *single lone mothers.* Also concealed by the shared label 'single lone mother' was the fact that seven were, or had been in, other relationships since the one with the father of their child(ren). Nor – for three mothers – did their single lone motherhood preclude either a good continuing relationship with their child's father (even though they were not living with them) or hopes of future cohabitation and possible marriage. Moreover, the 12 survey mothers who were *cohabiting* or *married* at the time of interview included three women who were living with a partner who was not the father of their child.

The mothers experiences were compared with those of a group of eight teenage women who were sexually active but childless.

Economic factors

Responses to out of marriage conceptions have changed at a time when the opportunities for young people to support themselves and a family through work have radically altered.[3] By 1994, only a half of teenage men and 7 out of 10 of those in their early twenties were in employment;[4] one in five young men aged 16-19 and one in seven of those aged 20-29 were unemployed.[5] While youth wages, no longer protected by wages councils, have fallen in recent years,[6] the proportion of young people who are in education or training has increased.

The result, has been a diminishing proportion of young men with independent incomes from employment. This points to one of the reasons that young men may be unwilling or unable to assume the financial responsibility of fatherhood. It also suggests a reason why young women may have ceased to view them as suitable partners, husbands and fathers.[7] In the present study few of the fathers living apart from their children appeared to be in regular, full-time jobs.

Housing

It also appeared that family formation had been made more difficult, for some, because of problems obtaining access to independent housing. Mothers – both single and cohabiting – had found that they were not allowed to put their names on the waiting list for a council house until they were 18 years old. Even then, they were given to understand that they might still face a long wait. Living with parents – either their own or those of the fathers – was not always an option. Where it was, it could work well in the short-term but it was rarely an ideal arrangement long-term and relationships had been placed under stress. Despite this, none had declared themselves homeless and temporary bed and breakfast accomodation had been offered to only one couple. They considered it a poor foundation for securing their relationship.

All this may appear a shade ironic given assertions that one of the reasons teenage women become pregnant is to jump the housing queue. It is a claim that persists despite the evidence that:

- most teenage conceptions are accidental;[8]

- mothers under 18 are not usually allowed to put their names on local authority housing waiting lists;[9]

- teenage mothers are not generally knowledgeable about access to housing;[10]

- where teenage mothers are housed, it is not at the expense of two-parent families with children.[11]

Certainly, none of the young mothers in the present study could be said to have 'got pregnant to get a council flat'. It was however, evident that some of the women who were cohabiting at the time of interview would have benefited from housing policies that made it easier to establish and sustain themselves as a family unit. Such policies might also have helped some of the single lone mothers to sustain relationships with the fathers of their children which subsequently failed.

Sexual activity and conception

Earlier physical maturation,[12] peer and societal pressures[13] and confused social messages about sex and sexual activity[14] are numbered among the possible explanations for an historical fall in age at first intercourse[15] and increasing sexual activity among young people.[16] Among all but a few of the young mothers in this study, first intercourse had occurred before they were 17 and half had conceived within a year of that experience. Which is not to suggest that youthful sexual activity is as widespread as sometimes assumed. Most young people, for example, do not have sexual intercourse before they are legally of age.[17] Nor is the current level of conceptions and births to teenage women as high as it was 20 years ago.[18] There are more than 40,000 *fewer* births to teenage women than in the mid 1970s (See Chapter 2. Box 1). Even so, teenage fertility rates in Britain did not decline in the 1980s in the way that they did in other European countries.[19]

Some attempts to explain this disparity have sought to implicate the wider availability of sex education. Such assumptions are challenged by international evidence,[20] including the lower rates of teenage pregnancy in countries with significant sex education programmes and where contraceptives are widely available. Research suggests, moreover, that sex education does not lead to increased sexual activity and may delay rather than encourage first intercourse – as well as encouraging safer sexual practices.[21] Programmes which combine knowledge of the reproductive process, information about contraception and advise postponement of sexual activity are more effective than those which teach abstinence alone.[22] Attempts to make sex education the culprit for teenage sexual experimentation, moreover, tend to overlook the other influences on young people, including the powerful and prolific messages about sexual activity that young people receive from the media and advertising. Teenagers may perceive these as suggesting that they are abnormal if they are *not* sexually active.[23]

A number of the young women in the present study did, indeed, mention the pressure they had encountered from their peers – both girls and boys – to engage in sexual activity. When they had done so, their sex education, or what they remembered of it, and the attendant difficulties of obtaining and correctly using contraceptives within a developing relationship did not guarantee against conception. The teenage women seemed both better informed about sexual activity and its consequences and more confident in handling their sexual relationships.

Previous research suggests that contraceptive use at first intercourse increases with age and 'planned' sexual intercourse and is more likely with a regular partner. Higher educational attainment is also associated with becoming sexually active later rather than earlier and with a greater use of contraception.[24] However, as many as a half of the mothers in the FPSC study reported having used some form of contraception at first intercourse. All but one of the teenage women had done so. It could, therefore, be argued that the greatest risks of conception arose from the unplanned and infrequent nature of youthful sexual behaviour. Pregnancies were often the result of inconsistent[25] or incorrect use of contraceptives, (such as sickness, diarrhoea or antibiotics rendering the pill ineffective) rather than failure to use contraceptives at all (only four mothers who did not want to conceive had never used contraceptives).

It was not uncommon for mothers to experience difficulty in obtaining contraception. They met a range of barriers including, their own embarrassment and anxieties about confidentiality, parental disapproval, medical reluctance, cost and lack of access. There was no suggestion at all from the study that access to contraception had encouraged promiscuous sexual activity. This was true even of the small number of women who had been prescribed the contraceptive pill at an early age because of their irregular or painful periods.

Keeping the baby

Another theory about teenage parenthood is that as opportunities for paid employment decline, so young people try to achieve adult status through earlier sexual activity and parenthood. Once teenage mothers have conceived, it is argued, their limited education prospects and employment opportunities encourage them to continue with the pregnancy.[26]

While a subliminal role cannot be ruled out, this was not an explanation that the mothers actually gave for becoming pregnant and deciding to remain so. The most obvious and potent factor was their opposition to abortion. This accords with other studies that have found a tendency for teenagers to be more opposed to abortion than older women and for anti-abortion feelings to be stronger in lower than higher social class communities.[27] A study in Scotland,[28] for example, found higher conception rates and lower abortion rates in poorer socio-economic areas and the reverse in better off neighbourhoods. Such a connection still leaves open the possibility that the way teenage women respond to conception reflects a *combination* of their attitudes to abortion and an assessment of their future prospects.[29]

When deciding how to respond to their pregnancy, the young women were also influenced by the attitudes of their peers and their parents – although decisions to 'keep the baby' had sometimes been taken in spite of advice from family members to seek a termination. Some of the mothers also expressed anxiety about attitudes within their local community. They believed there was greater stigma attached to having an abortion than to becoming a single lone mother. Two women had decided to continue with a pregnancy with the experience of a previous abortion behind them. But there were also a few mothers who expressed a wish, with hindsight, that they had agreed to a termination. Two others described circumstances in which they would consider an abortion in the future.

Young women, of course, are less likely to choose abortion if it has not been presented to them as an option at a sufficiently early stage. The interviews in this study suggest that not all the women had the opportunity to make such a free and informed choice.[30] It is, moreover, an emotionally charged decision and imminent compared with the more distant and positive choice of motherhood.

Policy issues

This study was not concerned 'directly' with the social security costs of single lone motherhood. Rather it hoped to shed light on the underlying influences on the formation of single lone mother families. Its aim in doing so was to inform policy development which is understandably directly concerned with public expenditure costs.

Teenage pregnancies

Without school sex education, some of the mothers in the present study would probably have received no reliable information about

human reproduction and contraception at all. The evidence in this and other studies is, even so, that sex education programmes in some schools are poorly matched with the perceptions, development and behaviour of young people.[31] They may know, for example, that unprotected sexual activity can lead to conception, but still not have any real appreciation of the chances that it will happen to them or know how to put their theoretical knowledge into practice within their youthful relationships.[32] Like a number of the young mothers described in this report, they may take risks and engage in unprotected intercourse in the mistaken belief that getting pregnant is 'something that happens to other people'.[33]

All pupils should have access to the basic biological study of human reproduction as part of the science curriculum. Following the Education Act 1993, it is also compulsory for maintained secondary schools to provide sex education. The only curriculum components that are specified, however, are the study of HIV/AIDS and other sexually transmitted diseases. Thus it remains up to individual schools whether they include such aspects as contraception and abortion or the broader aspects of sex education, such as relationships, parental responsibilities and family life. Parents, moreover, have been given the right to withdraw their children from sex education classes. Some health professionals fear that it may be the most vulnerable who will be withdrawn including those who have no other reliable source of sex education and those who are being sexually abused.

Experts agree that children and young people can best benefit from a combination of advice and teaching about sex provided by parents and by schools. Either source of information, on its own, is less likely to meet all of a young person's needs.[34] However, the likelihood – underlined by the mothers in this study – that a proportion of pupils will either miss classes or fail to absorb the relevant messages argues the need for additional sources of information and advice that can easily be accessed by young people.

The thorny issue of what should be taught also needs to be addressed. The experience of the survey mothers accords with that of health education professionals, who have argued in favour of a broadly-based approach. Basic knowledge about human reproduction and contraception are, put another way, only half the story. Classes should pay attention to wider questions of self esteem and assertiveness, encouraging young people to keep control in personal relationships and enable them to say 'no' when they want to, or to engage in sexual activity safely if they so choose.

The issue of access to contraception also needs to be addressed. One result of the *Health of the Nation* target of reducing the under 16 conception rate has been an increase in family planning services directed to or dedicated for young people.[35] Data from the Family Planning Association already report that use of clinics is increasing among teenagers. Their calculations suggest that the prevention of pregnancies is cost effective.[36]

For some teenagers, no matter how dismayed they may be to discover they are pregnant, the option of having a baby more than seven months hence will seem an emotionally less difficult choice than agreeing immediately to an abortion.[37] Moreover, if the strong anti-abortion sentiments expressed by some of the mothers in this study apply to a proportion of all young women, then it is clear that if the problem of unplanned, unwanted teenage pregnancies is to be effectively addressed, it must tackled before conception, not after.

Single lone motherhood

There is a danger that policy-making with regard to single lone motherhood will be unduly influenced by two mistaken assumptions:

- that unplanned conceptions always imply unwanted babies;

- that the disadvantaged start faced by many single lone mothers and their babies precludes all possibility of resilience and outcomes that eventually prove satisfactory.

Teenagers' conceptions are less likely to have been planned than those of older women. But that does not necessarily prevent them from eventually taking pleasure in their pregnancy, their babies and motherhood.[38] Although most of the mothers interviewed for this study had not planned for their family lives to take the course they did and would have done things differently given a second chance, they certainly would *not* have parted with their children once they had been born.[39]

In the United States, Frank Furstenberg has observed the diverse experiences of adolescent mothers and stressed the importance of policy-making which makes positive outcomes more likely.[40] The question raised is how to help single, lone mothers to develop and prosper (and their children likewise) as well as increase their self-sufficiency without creating perverse incentives

for more young women to follow the same course. Education, training and employment measures that increase the confidence of young people in their future prospects may be linked to postponed parenthood. It would also make sense, however, if policies for preventing unplanned conceptions were matched by further learning, skills training and job opportunities for those young women who continue to find themselves raising children on their own.

All the mothers interviewed for this study said they planned to find paid work once their children were in school. But there was a gap between their aspirations and their general lack of qualifications, skills or work experience. They could, under existing social security regulations, combine low paid part-time work (of less than 16 hours a week) with continued receipt of Income Support; but such work would be an unlikely launchpad to financial self-sufficiency. For those contemplating longer hours, the combination of lost benefits and added costs of childcare, travel to work, tax and national insurance continue to create a powerful 'poverty trap'.[41] The prospects of escape from dependency are made harder still by the financial hardship and debt which often accompanies single lone motherhood and the insecurities which mothers face in the transition from benefit to paid work.[42]

A few of the interview mothers had already looked for jobs and concluded that employment, for the time being, was not an option because opportunities were limited or childcare unavailable. The majority, however, seemed to take it for granted that they would stay at home with their children until they reached compulsory school age. It is difficult to know whether greater incentives to acquire qualifications and skills and to take full or part-time work would have altered this disposition. There could, however, be no doubt as to their forthcoming need for such incentives if their aspirations are ever to be fulfilled and those mothers to become economically independent. Much, even then, will depend on the availability of labour market opportunities and accessibility and affordability of child care.

Recent public debate and developments in social policy rarely allow that relationships, their formation and survival are issues of concern to single lone mothers. This qualitative study suggests otherwise. Housing and employment, moreover, are essential for such family life and neither were sufficiently available to the mothers and fathers; there might have been different outcomes for some of the teenage parents if they had been.

Notes

1 Estimates suggest that between a third and a half of <u>all</u> pregnancies are not planned. See Brook Advisory Centres, Annual Report 1993-94 and *Family Planning Today* (1994) Family Planning Association, fourth quarter.

2 See Chapter 2.

3 Kiernan, K.E. (1995).

4 Department of Employment Gazette, June 1995.

5 Central Statistical Office (1995).

6 Unemployment Unit and Youthaid Brief, November/ December 1993.

7 See, for example, House of Commons Social Security Committee (1995), Coleman, J.C. (1993) and Jones, G. et al (1992).

8 See, for example, Simms, M. and Smith, C. (1986), Hudson, F. and Ineichen, B. (1991) and Phoenix, A. (1991).

9 See Chapter 7.

10 Clark, E. (1989).

11 Institute of Housing (1991).

12 Measured, for example, by the age at which girls start to menstruate. See, Curtis, H. et al (1988) and Johnson, A. et al (1994).

13 See, for example, Lees, S. (1993), Moore, S. and Rosenthal, S. (1993) and Scally, G. (1993).

14 See, for example, Jones, E. (1985) and Spencer, B. (1984).

15 Age at first intercourse has fallen from 21 years for women now aged 55-59 to 17 years for those aged 16-24. (Johnson, A. et al, 1994).

16 See, for example, Moore, S. and Rosenthal, S. (1993), Ford, N. (1987), Bone, M. (1986), Bury, J. (1984), Dunnel, K. (1979), Farrell, C. (1978) and Schofield, M. (1968).

17 Just over a quarter (27 per cent) of young men and less than one in five (17 per cent of) young women now aged between 16 and 24 had their first experience of sexual intercourse before they were sixteen years old. (Johnson, A. et al, 1994).

18 Babb, P. (1995).

19 Kiernan,K. (1995).

20 Jones, E. (1985).

21 Baldo, M. et al (1993) and Oakley, A. et al, (1995).

22 Allen, I. (1987).

23 Mellanby, A. (1992) and Curtis, H.A. (1988).

24 Johnson, A. et al (1994).

25 National data suggests that contraceptive use by young people is commonly low at first intercourse and by no means always consistent thereafter. See, for example, Family Planning Association (1992) and Simms, M. and Smith, C. (1986).

26 Moore, S. and Rosenthal, D. (1993).

27 Johnson, A. et al (1994) and Hudson, F. and Ineichen, B. (1991).

28 Smith, T. (1993).

29 Johnson, A. et al, (1994).

30 Hadley, A. (1994), Birch, D. (1992) and Simms, M. and Smith, C. (1986).

31 Phelps, F.A. et al (1994), Lopes, L. (1993) 'Reasons and Resources: The human side of risk taking' in Bell, N.J. and Bell, R.W., and Ingham, R. (1993).

32 Millstein, S. (1993) 'Perceptual, attributional, and affective processed perceptions of vulnerability through the life span', in Bell, N.J. and Bell, R.W. (Eds) *Adolescent Risk Taking.*

33 See also Munday, K. (1993) and Mellanby, A. et al (1993).

34 Allen, I. (1987).

35 Secretary of State for Health (1991) and (1992).

36 Family Planning Association (1992), *Family Planning Today* (1995), Second Quarter and additional information provided by the Association.

37 See also Hudson, F. (1993).

38 Munday, K. (1993), Family Planning Association and Middlesex University (1993) and Simms, M. and Smith, C. (1986).

39 Munday, K. (1993).

40 Furstenberg, F. et al (1981).

41 Wilcox, S. (1993) and Burghes, L. (1993).

42 Burghes, L. (1993).

Methodological notes on the qualitative research

1) Social and Community Planning Research recruited and interviewed the mothers and young women in 1944. Interviews took place in Doncaster, Fareham, London, Manchester and Plymouth. Interviews were typically just under an hour and a half long. The interviews were tape recorded and the verbatim transcripts analysed by Louie Burghes.

2) The three comparison groups were defined as follow:

Teenage single lone mothers (19)

a. Must have been teenagers at the birth of their (first) child.

b. They may have cohabited at some time with the child's father (before or after conception or birth) or some other partner but must not be cohabiting at selection.

c. They must never have been married.

d. They may be living on their own, or with their own parents or as part of another household.

Teenage mothers in cohabiting partnerships (12)

a. Must have been teenagers at the birth of their (first) child.

b. They must be cohabiting with (and may be married to) either the father of the (reference) child or with another partner.

c. They do not have to have been cohabiting at the time of the conception or birth of the child.

d. They could have married between conception and birth.

Teenage girls (8)

a. Must have been at 'risk of conception', defined as at least one experience of sexual intercourse.

b. They could be cohabiting with (but not married to) a partner.

Additional information from the research

Some of the subject areas discussed with the young mothers taking part in the qualitative research yielded too little information to merit inclusion in the main text of this report. In particular, the women did not, or could not, report fully about their own family backgrounds and those of the fathers of their children. The limited material that was obtained can be described under three headings:

- family fertility patterns;

- mothers' experience of family life;

- fathers' backgrounds.

Family fertility patterns

The fertility patterns of the mothers' own mothers were explored in the light of their daughters' responses to their own conceptions.

Most of the mothers of the single lone mothers had had their first child in their teens. The age range was from 16 – two births – to an outlying single birth at 27 years. About a quarter were married before conception and a half married after conception (whether before or after the birth).

One mother's mother had cohabited until the father left when the respondent was 2 years old; another mother's mother had been forced to give up her child for adoption.

Age at first birth was spread over an even narrower age range for the cohabiting mother's mothers – 16 to 21 years.

Like the mothers of the single mothers, the most common family formation pattern of the mothers of the cohabiting mothers, was marriage following conception or birth (rather than preceding it). Two of these mothers had married before conception. Two couples had never married and the mothers had married a subsequent partner. One mother had never done

so and was reported by her daughter to have said *"...it's the worst mistake of your life getting married."* [2]

Mothers' experience of family life

Nearly half the single lone mothers and two thirds of the cohabiting mothers had experienced disruption within their own families while growing up. This mostly related to the breakdown of their parents relationship – in some cases becoming part of a stepfamily – although there were two women who had been placed in care. (One woman who did not get on with her stepfather had voluntarily placed herself in care – her foster father was, however, the father of her child).

In spite of having birth parents who had separated, a number described their families as happy and loving:

"we sort it out...they're that kind hearted." [2]

"...it was just me, my mum and my stepdad and I was getting quite spoilt and I really enjoyed it and we were very close me and my Mum." [2]

But there were also women whose home lives had generally been unhappy. They included those who had seen their fathers assault their mothers or had, themselves, been abused.

"My Mum and Dad didn't care really for me." [1] (Physically abused daughter)

"...we didn't do homework at home; we used to sit at school so that we didn't get thumped when we got in and there was so much rowing going on at home." [1]

Eight mothers had, as a result, spent part of their childhood living with their grandmothers (5) or in local authority care (3).

Fathers

The mothers were asked about the ages and employment histories of the fathers of their children and whether these had influenced their relationships and living arrangements.

In the case of cohabiting mothers, the fathers had mostly been in their late teens and early twenties at the time their babies were born. Nine of the 12 were in work. Of the three who were unemployed, two were no longer in a relationship with the mother.

The ages of the men who had fathered the children of the single lone mothers were more varied. In addition to those in their late teens, there were at least three school-age fathers, two in their mid-20s and two in their 30s or 40s.

Not all the mothers knew much about their employment histories, but it appeared that just over a third had been in work – although often only intermittently. Three were still at school or had just left when their babies were born, two were chronically sick and at least one was unemployed.

Bibliography

Allen, I. (1987) *Education in sex and personal relationships,* Policy Studies Institute.

Allen, I. (1991) *Family Planning and Pregnancy Counselling Projects for Young People,* Policy Studies Institute.

Babb, P. (1993) 'Teenage conceptions and fertility in England and Wales, 1971-91', *Population Trends,* No 74, HMSO.

Babb, P. (1995) 'Birth Statistics 1993', *Population Trends,* No 79, HMSO.

Babb, P. and Bethune, A. (1995) 'Trends in births outside marriage', *Population Trends,* No 81, HMSO.

Baldo, M., Aggleton, P. and Slutkin, G. (1993) *Does Sex Education lead to earlier or increased sexual activity in youth?,* WHO Global programme on AIDS, Geneva, Switzerland.

Bell, N.J. and Bell, R.W. (Editors) (1993) *Adolescent Risk Taking,* Sage Publications.

Birch, D.M.L. (1992) *"Are you my sister, Mummy",* Youth Support Publications.

Bone, M. (1985) *Family Planning in Scotland in 1982,* HMSO.

Bone, M. (1986) 'Trends in single women's sexual behaviour in Scotland', *Population Trends.*

Bradshaw, J. and Millar, J. (1991) *Lone Parent Families in the UK,* Department of Social Security, Research Report No.6, HMSO.

Bradshaw, J. and Millar, J. (1994) 'Lone mothers: family, employment and benefit changes', *Benefits,* Issue 9.

Brown, A. (1986) 'Family Circumstances of young children', *Population Trends,* No. 43, HMSO.

Burghes, L. (1993), *One parent families, Policy Options for the 1990s,* Joseph Rowntree Foundation.

Burghes, L. (1994) 'Teenage sex and sex education', *Family Policy Studies Bulletin.*

Bury, J. (1984) 'Teenage Pregnancy in Britain', *Birth Control Trust.*

Bury, J. (1986) 'Teenagers and contraception', *British Journal of Family Planning.*

Central Statistical Office (1995) *Social Trends 25,* OPCS, HMSO.

Church, J. and Summerfield, C. (1994) *Social Focus on Children,* Central Statistical Office, HMSO.

Clark, E. (1989) *Young single mothers today: A qualitative study of the housing and support needs,* National Council for One Parent Families.

Clark, E. and Coleman, J. (1991) *Growing up Fast. A follow up study of teenage mothers in adult life,* Trust for the Study of Adolesence.

Coleman, J.C. (1993) 'Understanding Adolesence Today: A Review', *Children and Society,* 7:2.

Cooper, J. (1991) 'Births outside marriage: recent trends and associated demographic and social change', *Population Trends,* No. 70, HMSO.

Curtis, H.A., Lawrence, C.J. and Tripp, J.H. (1988) 'Teenage sexual intercourse and pregnancy', *Archives of Diseases in Childhood,* 63.

Curtis, H.A., Lawrence, C.J., and Tripp, J.H. (1989) 'Teenage sexuality: the implications for controlling AIDS', *Archives of Diseases in Childhood,* 64.

Curtis, H.A., Tripp, J.H., Lawrence, C.J. and Clarke, W.L. (1988) 'Teenage relationships and sex education', *Archives of Diseases in Childhood,* 63.

Dean, M. (1993) 'Targeting teenage single mothers', *The Lancet,* Volume 342.

Department of Social Security (1993), *The Growth of Social Security,* HMSO.

Department of Social Security (1994) *Social Security Statistics,* HMSO.

Donovan, C. (1990) 'Adolescent Sexuality', *British Medical Journal,* Volume 300.

Dunnel, K. (1979) *Family Formation 1976,* HMSO.

Ermisch, J. (1989) *The duration of lone Parenthood in Britain,* CEPR Discussion Paper, Number 303.

Ermisch, J. (forthcoming) *Pre-marital cohabitation, childbearing and the creation of one parent families,* ESRC Research Centre working paper, University of Essex.

Estaugh, V. and Wheatley, J. (1990) *Family planning and family well-being,* Family Policy Studies Centre.

Family Planning Association (1992) *Young People: sexual attitudes and behaviour,* Factsheet 5B.

Family Planning Association (1994) *Teenage Opinion Survey,* Press Pack, 29 March.

Family Planning Association and Middlesex University (1993) *Children who have children.*

Family Policy Studies Centre (1994) 'Families and the Law', *Family Report 1.*

Farber, N. (1989) 'The significance of aspirations among unmarried women', *Social Service Review.*

Farrell, C. (1978) *My Mother Said ...,* Routledge.

Ford, N. (1987) 'Family Planning and Society. Research into heterosexual behaviour with implications for the spread of AIDS', *British Journal of Family Planning,* Volume 13.

Furstenberg, F. Jr, Brooks-Gun, J. and Philip Morgan, S. (1987) *Adolescent Mothers in later life,* Human Development in Cultural and Historical Contexts, Cambridge University Press.

Hadley, A. (1994) *Annual Report 1993-94,* Brook Advisory Centres.

Haskey, J. (1983) 'Marital status before marriage and age at marriage: their influence on the chance of divorce', *Population Trends,* No.32, HMSO.

Haskey, J. (1991) 'Estimated numbers and demographic characteristics of one-parent families in Great Britain', *Population Trends,* No.65, HMSO.

Haskey, J. (1993) 'Trends in the number of one-parent families in Great Britain', *Population Trends,* No. 71, HMSO.

Haskey, J. (1994) 'Estimated numbers of one-parent families and their prevalance in Great Britain 1991', *Population Trends,* No.78, HMSO.

House of Commons Social Security Committee, *Low Income Statistics: Low Income Families 1989-1992,* HMSO, 1995.

Hudson, F. (1993) *Too Much Too Young,* Teenage Parenthood Regional Conference, Doncaster.

Hudson, F. and Ineichen, B. (1991) *Taking it Lying Down. Sexuality and Teenage Motherhood,* Macmillan.

Ingham, Dr.R. (1993) '*Sexual Lifestyles of Young People',* paper given at Institute for Health Policy Studies conference, 'Preventing Teenage Pregnancy', University of Sourthampton.

Institute of Housing (1993) *One parent families – are they jumping the housing queue?*

Johnson, A, M., Wadsworth, J., Wellings, K. and Field, J. (1994) *Sexual Attitudes and Lifestyles,* Blackwell Scientific Publications.

Jones, E.J. et al (1985) 'Teenage pregnancy in developed countries: determinants and policy implications', *Family Planning Perspectives.*

Jones, G. and Wallace, C. (1992) *Youth, family and Citizenship,* Oxford University Press.

Kiernan, K.E. (1986) 'Teenage marriage and marital breakdown: a longitudinal study', *Population Studies,* No. 40.

Kiernan, K.E. (1995) *Transitions to parenthood: young mothers, young fathers – associated factors and later life experiences,* Welfare State Programme, WSP/113, STICERD, London School of Economics.

Kiernan, K.E. and Estaugh. V. (1993) *Cohabitation. Extra-marital childbearing and social policy,* Family Policy Studies Centre.

Land, H. (1995) *Paying for Care?,* in Bayley, R. et al (eds) *Policies for families: work, poverty and resources,* Family Policy Studies Centre.

Lees, S. (1986) *Losing Out: sexuality and adolescent girls,* Hutchinson.

Lees, S. (1993) *Sugar and Spice,* Penguin.

McKay, S. and Marsh, A. (1994) *Lone Parents and Work,* Research Report No. 25, Department of Social Security, HMSO.

McRae, S. (1993) *Cohabiting Mothers. Changing marriage and motherhood,* Policy Studies Institute.

Mellanby, A., Phelps, F. and Tripp, J.H. (1992) 'Sex education more is not enough', *Journal of Adolescence,* 15.

Mellanby, A., Phelps, F. and Tripp, J.H. (1993) 'Teenagers, sex and risk taking', *British Medical Journal,* 307.

M. Mills (1979) *Pregnant at School: Joint Working Party on Pregnant School girls and Schoolgirl Mothers,* National Council for One Parent Families.

Moore, S. and Rosenthal, D. (1993) *Sexuality in Adolescence,* Trust for the Study of Adolescence.

Munday, K. (1993) 'Why teenagers get pregnant', *Primary Health Care.*

Oakley, A., Fullerton, D., Holland, J., Arnold, D., France-Dawson, M., Kelley. P., and McGrellis, S. (1995) 'Sexual health education interventions for young people: a methodological review', *British Medical Journal,* Volume 310, 21 January, pp 158-162.

Office of Population Censuses and Surveys (1987) *Birth Statistics 1837-1983,* FM1 no. 13, HMSO.

Office of Population Censuses and Surveys (1993) *General Household Survey 1991,* HMSO.

Office of Population Censuses and Surveys (1994a) *Birth Statistics 1992,* Series FM1 no. 21, HMSO.

Office of Population Censuses and Surveys (1994b) *Marriage and Divorce Statistics 1992,* Series FM2. no. 20, HMSO.

Office of Population Censuses and Surveys (1995a) *Conceptions in England and Wales, 1992,* OPCS Monitor, FM1 95/2, London, HMSO.

Office of Population Censuses and Surveys (1995b) *Marriage and Divorce Statistics 1993,* Series FM2 no 21, London, HMSO.

Office of Population Censuses and Surveys (1995c) *Birth Statistics 1993,* Series FM1 no 22, London, HMSO.

Phelps, F.A., Mellanby, A.R., Crichton, N.J. and Tripp, J.H. (1994) 'Sex education: the effect of a peer programme on pupils (aged 13-14 years) and their peer leaders', *Health Education Journal,* 53.

Phoenix, A. (1991) *Young Mothers?,* Polity Press.

Reid, A. (1994) *A woman's right to choose,* YWCA seminar on the special needs of young women.

Rimmer, L. (1981) *Families in Focus,* Study Commission on the Family.

Roll, J. (1990) *Young People,* Factsheet 5, Family Policy Studies Centre.

Russell, J.K. (1988) 'Early Teen Pregnancy', *Maternal and Child Health.*

Scally, Dr. G. (1993) 'Pregnancies – the challenge of prevention', Sir William Power Memorial lecture 1992, *Midwives Chronicle.*

Schofield, M. (1968) *The Sexual Behaviour of Young People,* Pelican.

Secretary of State for Health (1991) *The Health of the Nation. A Consultative Document for Health in England,* Cm 1523, HMSO.

Secretary of State for Health (1992) *A Strategy for Health in England,* Cm 1986, HMSO.

Simms, M. and Smith, C. (1986) *Teenage mothers and their partners,* Research Report No 15, Department of Health and Social Security, HMSO.

Smith, T. (1993) 'Influence of socioeconomic factors on attaining targets for reducing teenage pregnancies', *British Medical Journal,* 306.

Speak, S., Cameron, S., Woods, R. and Gilroy, R. (1995) *Young single mothers: the barriers to independent living,* Family and Parenthood, Policy and Practice, Family Policy Studies Centre.

Spencer, B. (1984) 'Young men: their attitudes towards sexuality and birth control', *The British Journal of Family Planning,* Volume 10.

Ward, C., Dale, A., and Joshi, H. (1994) *Combining employment with childcare: an escape from dependence,* Social Statistics Research Unit, City University, Working Paper 38.

Wilcox, S. (1993) *Higher rents and work disincentives,* Findings No.93, Joseph Rowntree Foundation.

Witner, M. (1993a) 'Health of infants born to teenage mothers affected more by family background than by mother's age', *Family Planning Perspectives.*

Witner, M. (1993b) 'Pregnancy risk lessened for teenagers with high education aspirations', *Family Planning Perspectives.*

Wolkind, S.N. and Kruk, S. (1985) 'Teenage Pregnancy and Motherhood', *Journal of the Royal Society of Medicine.*

Family & Parenthood Policy & Practice

Excluding primary school children

Diet, choice and poverty

Social, cultural and nutritional aspects of food consumption among low-income families

Family support for young people

CARL PARSONS with LOUISE BENNS, JEAN HAILES and KEITH HOWLETT

B. DOBSON, A. BEARDSWORTH, T. KEIL AND R. WALKER

GILL JONES

Family & Parenthood Policy & Practice

Family & Parenthood Policy & Practice

Family & Parenthood Policy & Practice

Excluding primary school children by *Carl Parsons et al.*
An urgent, focused evaluation of the effect of exclusion as experienced by children, their families, and those drawn into the management of the situation in an official capacity.
A4; 64pp; ISBN 0 907051 76 6; £9.50. November 1994.

Diet, choice and poverty:
Social, cultural and nutritional aspects of food consumption among low-income families by *Barbara Dobson et al.*
A detailed description of the food-related ideas, preferences, priorities and choices of those living on low incomes. The study pays attention to the sources of information about food, patterns of purchasing, consumption and distribution within the household and adaptations to low income.
A4; 36pp; ISBN 0 907051 75 8; £7.50. November 1994.

Family support for young people by *Gill Jones.*
A study that examines a group of young people's relationships with their families of origin as they make the transition to adult life.
A4; 36pp; ISBN 0 907051 78 2; £7.50. January 1995.

Nutrition and diet in lone-parent families in London

Young single mothers: barriers to independent living

ELIZABETH DOWLER and CLAIRE CALVERT

SUZANNE SPEAK, STUART CAMERON, ROBERTA WOODS and ROSE GILROY

Family & Parenthood Policy & Practice

Family & Parenthood Policy & Practice

Postage and packing

up to £5.00 **free**

£5.01 – £15.00 **add £1.50**

£15.01 – £25.00 **add £3.00**

£25.01 – £35.00 **add £4.50**

£35.01 & over **add £6.00**

Nutrition and diet in lone-parent families in London
by *Elizabeth Dowler and Claire Calvert.*
This study asks whether nutritional deprivation is also a part of the poverty so generally experienced by lone parent families, and investigates the strategies adopted by lone parents for making ends meet.
A4; 60pp; ISBN 0 907051 79 0; £9.50. February 1995.

Young single mothers by *Suzanne Speak et al.*
This research, centred on the City of Newcastle upon Tyne, investigates the barriers to independent living, as experienced by young, single never-married mothers, setting up their first independent homes, without the financial or practical assistance of a partner.
A4; 64pp; ISBN 0 907051 85 5; £9.50. July 1995.

PUBLISHED BY
Family Policy Studies Centre

SUPPORTED BY
JR JOSEPH ROWNTREE FOUNDATION

Published and distributed by Family Policy Studies Centre, 231 Baker Street, London NW1 6XE • Tel: 0171 486 8179 • Fax: 0171 224 3510